SUNFLY
MOST WANTED

sfmw 801

-

sfmw 932

IN ORDER OF SONG TITLE

When requesting a song write down

Your Name

The Song Name (eg. 2 minutes to midnight)

The Artist name (eg. Iron maiden)

The code (eg SFMW889)

the track number (eg. 02)

please make sure you have
all that information before handing to the DJ

SONG	ARTIST	MF CODE	TRACK
1234	Feist	SFMW894	01
18 Till I Die	Bryan Adams	SFMW803	11
18 Wheeler	Pink	SFMW886	01
18 Yellow Roses	Bobby Darin	SFMW876	12
2 Minutes To Midnight	Iron Maiden	SFMW889	02
25 Minutes To Go	Johnny Cash	SFMW846	15
26 Cents	Wilkinsons	SFMW892	14
29 Palms	Robert Plant	SFMW913	02
3 00 Am	Busted	SFMW853	06
4 Seasons Of Loneliness	Boyz 2 Men	SFMW932	10
57 Chevrolet	Billie Jo Spears	SFMW819	15
6 Underground	Sneaker Pimps	SFMW882	08
68 Guns	Alarm	SFMW889	03
Absolute	Scritti Politti	SFMW910	06
Across The Universe	Beatles	SFMW906	11
Affirmation	Savage Garden	SFMW804	02
After Dark	Tito And The Tarantulas	SFMW917	15
After The Love Has Gone	Earth Wind And Fire	SFMW814	07
Afternoon Delight	Starland Vocal Band	SFMW903	15
Afternoons And Coffee Spoons	Crash Test Dummies	SFMW877	08
Ain't Got No I Got Life	Nina Simone	SFMW863	02

Title	Artist	Code	#
Ain't No Doubt	Jimmy Nail	SFMW807	05
Ain't No Love In The Heart Of The C	Whitesnake	SFMW906	02
Ain't No Man	Dina Carroll	SFMW830	01
Ain't No Sunshine	Bill Withers	SFMW804	11
Ain't That A Kick In The Head	Dean Martin	SFMW921	14
Alfie	Dionne Warwick	SFMW819	10
Alive	Pearl Jam	SFMW886	10
All About Loving You	Bon Jovi	SFMW843	01
All About Soul	Billy Joel	SFMW823	13
All American Girl	Carrie Underwood	SFMW927	09
All And All	Joyce Sims	SFMW832	01
All At Once	Whitney Houston	SFMW820	08
All At Once	Whitney Houston	SFMW827	03
All By Myself	Celine Dion	SFMW852	03
All Cried Out	Alison Moyet	SFMW820	09
All Fired Up	Pat Benatar	SFMW888	12
All I Ask Of You	Phantom Of The Opera	SFMW806	08
All I Need	Air	SFMW877	15
All I Really Want	Alanis Morissette	SFMW839	02
All I Want	Wet Wet Wet	SFMW858	12
All I Want To Do	Sugarland	SFMW930	13

Title	Artist	Code
All In Your Mind	Mariah Carey	SFMW831 01
All Kinds Of Everything	Dana	SFMW898 10
All My Life	Foo Fighters	SFMW851 11
All Night Long	Rainbow	SFMW905 01
All Or Nothing	Small Faces	SFMW818 10
All Over Me	Josh Turner	SFMW930 14
All Sparks	Editors	SFMW925 05
All Stood Still	Ultravox	SFMW870 05
All The Times I Cried	Sharleen Spiteri	SFMW906 12
All These Things That I've Done	Killers	SFMW862 08
All This Love That I'm Giving	Gwen Mccrae	SFMW905 09
All You Do Is Bring Me Down	Mavericks	SFMW848 09
Almost There	Level 42	SFMW909 13
Alone	Glee Cast	SFMW924 15
Always On The Run	Lenny Kravitz	SFMW872 06
Amazed	Lonestar	SFMW802 01
American Girl	Tom Petty And The Heartbreake	SFMW923 11
American Idiot	Green Day	SFMW857 01
American Soldier	Toby Keith	SFMW850 10
And She Was	Talking Heads	SFMW884 04
And The Beat Goes On	Whispers	SFMW813 04
And The Beat Goes On	Whispers	SFMW831 02

Title	Artist	Code	
And Your Bird Can Sing	Beatles	SFMW896	10
Angel	Lionel Richie	SFMW843	15
Angel	Sarah Maclachlan	SFMW895	09
Angel Of Harlem	U2	SFMW813	15
Angelia	Richard Marx	SFMW829	01
Angelo	Brotherhood Of Man	SFMW834	01
Angels Wings	Westlife	SFMW815	13
Angels With Dirty Faces	Sham 69	SFMW893	06
Angie Baby	Helen Reddy	SFMW801	14
Animal	Def Leppard	SFMW896	14
Animal Crackers In My Soup	Shirley Temple	SFMW904	10
Animal Nitrate	Suede	SFMW895	06
Annie I'm Not Your Daddy	Kid Creole And The Coconuts	SFMW870	14
Another Brick In The Wall	Pink Floyd	SFMW848	10
Any Man Of Mine	Shania Twain	SFMW906	09
Any Old Iron	Stanley Holloway	SFMW909	08
Aqua Marina	Gary Miller	SFMW901	05
Aquarius Let The Sunshine In	5th Dimension	SFMW880	06
Are Friends Electric	Tubeway Army	SFMW801	05
Are Friends Electric	Tubeway Army	SFMW812	03
Are You Gonna Be My Girl	Jet	SFMW850	14

Title	Artist	Code	
Are You Gonna Go My Way	Tom Jones And Robbie Williams	SFMW829	02
Army Dreamers	Kate Bush	SFMW898	02
Army Of Me	Bjork	SFMW932	07
Arnold Layne	Pink Floyd	SFMW897	09
Around The Bend	Asteroids Galaxy Tour	SFMW920	02
Attention To Me	Nolans	SFMW902	09
Autobiography	Ashlee Simpson	SFMW873	03
Avalon	Roxy Music	SFMW832	02
Avenues And Alleyways	Tony Christie	SFMW859	14
Babooshka	Kate Bush	SFMW835	14
Baby Come Back	Player	SFMW914	12
Baby Come To Me	Patti Austin And James Ingram	SFMW846	11
Baby Girl	Sugarland	SFMW892	09
Baby Got Back	Sir Mix A Lot	SFMW897	07
Baby Grand	Billy Joel And Ray Charles	SFMW826	02
Baby I Don't Care	Jennifer Ellison	SFMW840	01
Baby I Don't Care	Transvision Vamp	SFMW897	08
Baby I Love You	Aretha Franklin	SFMW911	08
Back At One	Brian Mcknight	SFMW928	08
Back In Baby's Arms	Patsy Cline	SFMW868	12
Back In Black	Ac Dc	SFMW883	13
Back Round	Wolfmother	SFMW929	01

Title	Artist	Code	Track
Back To December	Taylor Swift	SFMW932	16
Bad Bad Boy	Nazareth	SFMW874	05
Bad Case Of Loving You	Robert Palmer	SFMW840	09
Bad Moon Rising	Creedence Clearwater Revival	SFMW871	04
Baker Street	Gerry Rafferty	SFMW860	02
Ballad Of Barry And Freda	Victoria Wood	SFMW826	03
Ballad Of John And Yoko	John Lennon	SFMW813	13
Ballerina Girl	Lionel Richie	SFMW836	07
Band On The Run	Wings	SFMW861	06
Bang Bang You're Dead	Dirty Pretty Things	SFMW923	04
Banquet	Bloc Party	SFMW925	06
Barbara Ann	Beach Boys	SFMW829	03
Barcelona	Freddie Mercury And Montserra	SFMW860	07
Barracuda	Heart	SFMW899	03
Basket Case	Green Day	SFMW849	04
Battle Of Who Could Care Less	Ben Folds Five	SFMW866	12
Beach Baby	First Class	SFMW802	12
Beat Goes On	Britney Spears	SFMW815	09
Beat It	Michael Jackson	SFMW861	04
Beat The Clock	Sparks	SFMW818	11
Beautiful Boy (Darling Boy)	John Lennon	SFMW824	11

Title	Artist	Code
Beautiful Girls	Sean Kingston	SFMW892 10
Beautiful Ones	Suede	SFMW848 15
Beautiful People	Marilyn Manson	SFMW883 04
Beautiful Soul	Jesse Maccartney	SFMW874 07
Beautiful Sunday	Daniel Boone	SFMW821 06
Because	Dave Clark Five	SFMW827 11
Because The Night	Patty Smyth	SFMW875 13
Becoming More Like Alfie	Divine Comedy	SFMW893 05
Bee Song (Busy Bee)	Arthur Askey	SFMW904 09
Beechwood 45789	Marvelettes	SFMW894 12
Been Caught Stealing	Jane's Addiction	SFMW875 10
Beetlebum	Blur	SFMW873 15
Begin The Beguine	Johnny Mathis	SFMW823 04
Behind Closed Doors	Charlie Rich	SFMW815 03
Behind The Mask	Eric Clapton	SFMW871 11
Being For The Benefit Of Mr Kite	Beatles	SFMW901 04
Belfast	Boney M	SFMW804 08
Bell Boy	Who	SFMW921 13
Ben	Michael Jackson	SFMW907 14
Best Things In Life Are Free	Janet Jackson And Luther Vand	SFMW812 08
Better Man	Thunder	SFMW880 11
Better Than This	Keane	SFMW910 03

Title	Artist	Code	Track
Beyond The Sea	Bobby Darin	SFMW860	11
Big Area	Then Jerico	SFMW873	12
Big Fun	Gap Band	SFMW844	01
Big Girls Don't Cry	Fergie	SFMW898	14
Big Gun	Ac Dc	SFMW932	01
Big Hunk O' Love	Elvis Presley	SFMW803	03
Big Love	Fleetwood Mac	SFMW836	03
Big River	Jimmy Nail	SFMW816	12
Big River	Johnny Cash	SFMW848	06
Big Rock Candy Mountain	Burl Ives	SFMW928	07
Big Sur	Thrills	SFMW846	13
Big Yellow Taxi	Joni Mitchell	SFMW890	09
Bike	Pink Floyd	SFMW920	10
Billie Jean	Michael Jackson	SFMW849	02
Billy Hunt	Jam	SFMW909	02
Birdhouse In Your Soul	They Might Be Giants	SFMW850	12
Birmingham Blues	Electric Light Orchestra	SFMW898	11
Bitter End	Placebo	SFMW841	08
Black And White Town	Doves	SFMW865	03
Black Cat	Janet Jackson	SFMW833	03
Black Hills Of Dakota	Doris Day	SFMW916	08

Title	Artist	Code
Black Hole Sun	Soundgarden	SFMW874 09
Black Horse And The Cherry Tree	Kt Tunstall	SFMW863 12
Blackbird	Beatles	SFMW925 03
Blame It On The Boogie	Jacksons	SFMW878 09
Blaydon Races	Jimmy Nail Tim Healy And Kevi	SFMW921 05
Bless Your Beautiful Hide	Howard Keel	SFMW905 11
Blind As A Bat	Meat Loaf	SFMW884 10
Blister In The Sun	Violent Femmes	SFMW849 14
Blood Sugar Sex Magik	Red Hot Chili Peppers	SFMW882 11
Bloody Well Right	Supertramp	SFMW884 05
Blower's Daughter	Damien Rice	SFMW860 06
Blowin' In The Wind	Bob Dylan	SFMW931 11
Blue	Leann Rimes	SFMW821 15
Blue Hotel	Chris Isaak	SFMW900 09
Blue Monday	New Order	SFMW868 06
Blues Power	Eric Clapton	SFMW838 02
Bohemian Like You	Dandy Warhols	SFMW839 14
Boot Scootin' Boogie	Brooks And Dunn	SFMW926 14
Born Of Frustration	James	SFMW900 02
Born Under A Bad Sign	Albert King	SFMW881 14
Borstal Breakout	Sham 69	SFMW889 04
Boss Drum	Shamen	SFMW885 03

Both Sides Now (2000 Version)	Joni Mitchell	SFMW892	12
Bourgeois Shangri La	Miss Li	SFMW918	03
Boy From New York City	Darts	SFMW828	01
Boy Named Sue	Johnny Cash	SFMW874	02
Boys Are Back In Town	Thin Lizzy	SFMW804	14
Boys Don't Cry	Cure	SFMW835	07
Branded Man	Merle Haggard	SFMW914	01
Brandy	O'jays	SFMW917	05
Brazen	Skunk Anansie	SFMW905	02
Break On Through To The Other Side	Doors	SFMW926	03
Break The Ice	Britney Spears	SFMW900	13
Breakfast In America	Supertramp	SFMW876	04
Breaking The Law	Judas Priest	SFMW892	01
Breathe	Faith Hill	SFMW836	12
Breathe	Pink Floyd	SFMW842	04
Brick	Ben Folds Five	SFMW839	10
Bridge Over Troubled Water	Simon And Garfunkel	SFMW864	01
Bring Me Sunshine	Morecambe And Wise	SFMW842	11
Bring Me To Life	Evanescence	SFMW840	02
Bring On The Dancing Horses	Echo And The Bunnymen	SFMW919	05
Broken	Seether And Amy Lee	SFMW858	04

Title	Artist	Code	#
Broken Arrow	Pixie Lott	SFMW929	07
Broken Down Angel	Nazareth	SFMW879	10
Brothers In Arms	Dire Straits	SFMW817	03
Brown Eyed Girl	Van Morrison	SFMW838	01
Brown Girl In The Ring	Boney M	SFMW809	14
Brown Sugar	Rolling Stones	SFMW820	05
Bubbles	Biffy Clyro	SFMW928	12
Buddy Holly	Weezer	SFMW851	02
Buffalo Soldier	Bob Marley	SFMW805	08
Buffalo Stance	Neneh Cherry	SFMW849	12
Bugsy Malone	Bugsy Malone	SFMW864	06
Bullets	Editors	SFMW874	13
Burning Heart	Survivor	SFMW904	01
By Your Side	Sade	SFMW877	14
Bye Bye	Jo Dee Messina	SFMW917	08
California	Joni Mitchell	SFMW829	04
California	Phantom Planet	SFMW858	05
California Blue	Roy Orbison	SFMW854	12
California Girls	Beach Boys	SFMW832	03
Call Me	Go West	SFMW868	07
Call Me	Spagna	SFMW890	10
Callin' Baton Rouge	Garth Brooks	SFMW924	14

Title	Artist	Code	Track
Calling All The Heroes	It Bites	SFMW842	01
Camouflage	Stan Ridgway	SFMW870	09
Can I Play With Madness	Iron Maiden	SFMW881	01
Can U Dig It	Mock Turtles	SFMW879	02
Can U Dig It	Pop Will Eat Itself	SFMW863	06
Can You Feel It	Jacksons	SFMW830	02
Candy	Paolo Nutini	SFMW917	03
Candy Girl	New Edition	SFMW842	03
Cannonball	Breeders	SFMW868	01
Cannonball	Damien Rice	SFMW918	04
Can't Fight This Feeling	Reo Speedwagon	SFMW849	05
Can't Get Enough (Of Your Love)	Bad Company	SFMW924	02
Can't Resist	Texas	SFMW871	12
Can't Stop Feeling	Franz Ferdinand	SFMW860	14
Can't Take My Eyes Off You	Andy Williams	SFMW815	08
Can't You Hear My Heartbeat	Herman's Hermits	SFMW877	11
Captain	Biffy Clyro	SFMW930	03
Captain Fantastic And The Brown Dir	Elton John	SFMW907	04
Captain Of Your Ship	Reparata And The Delrons	SFMW890	11
Car Wash	Rose Royce	SFMW807	13
Caravan Song	Barbara Dickson	SFMW821	03

Title	Artist	Code	Track
Carnival Girl	Texas	SFMW848	03
Carrie Ann	Hollies	SFMW895	12
Carry On Wayward Son	Kansas	SFMW875	06
Cat Crept In	Mud	SFMW822	01
Cat's In The Cradle	Harry Chapin	SFMW827	14
Cha Cha Slide	Dj Casper	SFMW851	05
Chain Reaction	Diana Ross	SFMW825	15
Chalk Dust	Bratt	SFMW833	04
Chantilly Lace	Big Bopper	SFMW816	07
Chapel Of Love	Dixie Cups	SFMW902	12
Chasing Rainbows	Shed Seven	SFMW869	09
Chattahoochee	Alan Jackson	SFMW821	02
Cheers	Cheers	SFMW803	05
Cheese And Onions	Rutles	SFMW912	08
Chequered Love	Kim Wilde	SFMW896	08
Chicken Fried	Zac Brown Band	SFMW928	03
Chicken Song	Spitting Image	SFMW835	04
Chihuahua	Dj Bobo	SFMW841	09
Children Of The Revolution	T Rex	SFMW805	13
Cigarettes And Alcohol	Oasis	SFMW869	04
Cinema Italiano	Kate Hudson ('nine' Soundtrac	SFMW921	10
Circle Of Life	Elton John	SFMW806	07

Title	Artist	Code	Track
Close To Me	Cure	SFMW856	02
Closer	Ne Yo	SFMW902	03
Closer To The Heart	Rush	SFMW905	15
Closest Thing To Crazy	Katie Melua	SFMW850	01
Cloudbusting	Kate Bush	SFMW879	04
Cocaine Blues	Johnny Cash	SFMW923	14
Cochise	Audioslave	SFMW865	15
Colour Of The Wind	Vanessa Williams	SFMW853	11
Come As You Are	Beverley Knight	SFMW877	10
Come As You Are	Nirvana	SFMW805	15
Come Away With Me	Norah Jones	SFMW837	14
Come Baby Come	K7	SFMW854	02
Come Back And Stay	Paul Young	SFMW834	02
Come Back My Love	Darts	SFMW818	15
Come Back Song	Darius Rucker	SFMW930	11
Come Back To What You Know	Embrace	SFMW867	07
Come Get Some	Rooster	SFMW856	05
Come Into My Life	Joyce Sims	SFMW832	04
Come Live With Me	Heaven 17	SFMW844	02
Comfortably Numb	Sciissor Sisters	SFMW872	13
Comin' Home Baby	Mel Torme	SFMW929	09

Title	Artist	Code	Track
Communication Breakdown	Roy Orbison	SFMW803	12
Concrete Schoolyard	Jurassic 5	SFMW883	07
Confidence Man	Jeff Healey	SFMW828	02
Confusion	Electric Light Orchestra	SFMW899	01
Connection	Elastica	SFMW845	09
Cool Rider (Grease 2)	Michelle Pfieffer	SFMW920	15
Cool Water	Frankie Laine	SFMW825	01
Cosmic Girl	Jamiroquai	SFMW846	05
Cosmic Love	Florence And The Machine	SFMW927	03
Could Have Told You So	Halo James	SFMW919	07
Could You Be Loved	Bob Marley	SFMW889	14
Court Of King Caractacus	Rolf Harris	SFMW844	03
Cover Me	Bruce Springsteen	SFMW836	05
Cover Of Rolling Stone	Dr Hook	SFMW819	13
Crash	Primitives	SFMW864	10
Creeque Alley	Mama's And Papa's	SFMW818	03
Criticize	Alexander O'neal	SFMW842	14
Crocodile Rock	Elton John	SFMW821	08
Cruel Summer	Bananarama	SFMW923	05
Crunchy Granola Suite	Neil Diamond	SFMW873	14
Cry	Sundays	SFMW909	10
Cry Little Sister (From The Lost Bo	Gerard Mcmann	SFMW913	15

Title	Artist	Code	
Cry To Me	Solomon Burke	SFMW864	11
Cry Wolf	A-ha	SFMW918	02
Cum On Feel The Noize	Slade	SFMW889	13
Cut Off	Kasabian	SFMW861	01
Cuts You Up	Peter Murphy	SFMW913	01
Daddy Cool	Boney M	SFMW808	01
Daddy Cool	Darts	SFMW820	04
Daddy Don't You Walk So Fast	Wayne Newton	SFMW823	05
Damn I Wish I Was Your Lover	Sophie B Hawkins	SFMW833	05
Dance Away	Roxy Music	SFMW907	13
Dance With My Father	Luther Vandross	SFMW855	04
Dance Yourself Dizzy	Liquid Gold	SFMW832	10
Dancin' In The Moonlight	Thin Lizzy	SFMW887	04
Dancing In The City	Marshall Hain	SFMW872	04
Dancing On My Own	Robyn	SFMW926	06
Dancing On The Ceiling	Lionel Richie	SFMW852	14
Dancing With Tears In My Eyes	Ultravox	SFMW812	13
Danger Games	Pinkees	SFMW870	07
Danger Zone	Kenny Loggins	SFMW859	09
Darkness	Darren Hayes	SFMW860	10
Darling	Frankie Miller	SFMW806	05

Title	Artist	Code	
Daughter	Pearl Jam	SFMW859	12
Day I Met Marie	Cliff Richard	SFMW825	11
Day In The Life	Beatles	SFMW859	05
Day Tripper	Beatles	SFMW850	04
Daydreamer	Menswear	SFMW894	04
Days Of Our Lives	Queen	SFMW835	16
Days Of Pearly Spencer	Marc Almond	SFMW868	15
Deadwood Stage	Doris Day	SFMW889	11
Dear Maria Count Me In	All Time Low	SFMW931	04
Dear Prudence	Siouxsie And The Banshees	SFMW839	01
Deck The Halls	Traditional (Big Band)	SFMW918	12
Deck The Rooftop	Glee Cast	SFMW930	01
Deeper The Love	Whitesnake	SFMW908	03
Delicate	Terence Trent D'arby And Des'	SFMW910	11
Demons	Fatboy Slim And Macy Gray	SFMW906	13
Denial Twist	White Stripes	SFMW932	03
Desire	U2	SFMW876	09
Desperado	Eagles	SFMW883	15
Destiny	Lionel Ritchie	SFMW866	08
Destiny	Zero 7	SFMW912	04
Detroit Rock	Citykiss	SFMW923	01
Devil Went Down To Georgia	Charlie Daniels	SFMW801	04

Title	Artist	Code	Track
Devil Woman	Marty Robbins	SFMW835	05
Diamonds Are A Girl's Best Friend	Marilyn Monroe	SFMW902	06
Diary Of Horrace Wimp	Electric Light Orchestra	SFMW835	08
Did You See Me Coming?	Pet Shop Boys	SFMW919	04
Dirty Cash	Adventures Of Stevie V	SFMW905	07
Dirty Diana	Michael Jackson	SFMW888	02
Dirty Love	Thunder	SFMW908	01
Dirty Old Town	Pogues	SFMW867	09
Do Anything You Wanna Do	Eddie And The Hot Rods	SFMW806	04
Do It To Me	Lionel Richie	SFMW818	09
Do That To Me One More Time	Captain And Tennille	SFMW924	10
Do The Bart Man	Simpsons	SFMW831	03
Do The Hucklebuck	Coast To Coast	SFMW826	04
Do Ya	Electric Light Orchestra	SFMW912	01
Do You Feel My Love	Eddy Grant	SFMW808	07
Do You Hear The People Sing?	Les Miserables	SFMW901	09
Do You Hear What I Hear	Bing Crosby	SFMW894	09
Do You Know What I Mean	Oasis	SFMW875	07
Doctor Beat	Miami Sound Machine	SFMW834	03
Dog Days Are Over	Florence And The Machine	SFMW925	09
Doin' The Do	Betty Boo	SFMW839	04

Title	Artist	Code	#
Dolce Vita	Ryan Paris	SFMW902	07
Dominos	Big Pink	SFMW920	01
Don't Believe In Is Anymore	Roger Whitaker	SFMW813	01
Don't Break My Heart	U B 40	SFMW812	12
Don't Come Around Here No More	Tom Petty And The Heartbreake	SFMW886	05
Don't Dream It's Over	Susan Boyle	SFMW932	05
Don't Fear The Reaper	Blue Oyster Cult	SFMW869	13
Don't Get Me Wrong	Pretenders	SFMW806	12
Don't Give Up	Peter Gabriel And Kate Bush	SFMW847	14
Don't Know Why	Norah Jones	SFMW837	15
Don't Leave Me Now	Elvis Presley	SFMW803	01
Don't Let Go	En Vogue	SFMW804	03
Don't Let It Go To Waste	Matt Willis	SFMW884	09
Don't Let Me Down	Beatles	SFMW824	08
Don't Look Back In Anger	Oasis	SFMW840	13
Don't Look Back Into The Sun	Libertines	SFMW856	08
Don't Lose My Number	Phil Collins	SFMW846	07
Don't Love You No More (I'm Sorry)	Craig David	SFMW877	09
Don't Make Me Wait	Bomb The Bass	SFMW888	10
Don't Mug Yourself	Streets	SFMW860	08
Don't Pay The Ferryman	Chris De Burgh	SFMW875	09

Title	Artist	Code	#
Don't Play That Song	Aretha Franklin	SFMW841	14
Don't Rain On My Parade	Bobby Darin	SFMW882	15
Don't Stop Believin'	Journey	SFMW917	13
Don't Stop Till You Get Enough	Michael Jackson	SFMW845	13
Don't Turn Around	Aswad	SFMW809	06
Don't Wanna Lose You	Gloria Estefan	SFMW809	12
Don't You Worry About A Thing	Stevie Wonder	SFMW830	03
Down On The Beach	Drifters	SFMW819	11
Dream A Little Dream Of Me	Mama's And Papa's	SFMW818	05
Dream Weaver	Gary Wright	SFMW892	08
Dreamer	Ozzy Osbourne	SFMW844	04
Dreaming My Dreams With You	Colleen Hewett	SFMW883	05
Dreaming Of You	Coral	SFMW853	12
Dreamlover	Mariah Carey	SFMW872	07
Dressed For Success	Roxette	SFMW804	09
Drift Away	Dobie Gray	SFMW932	17
Drifting	Sarah Mclachlan	SFMW914	15
Driftwood	Travis	SFMW802	02
Drink Drink Drink	Mario Lanza	SFMW902	05
Drive	Incubus	SFMW854	09
Driving With The Brakes On	Del Amitri	SFMW878	13
Drop The Pilot	Joan Armatrading	SFMW868	03

Title	Artist	Code	Track
Drops Of Jupiter	Train	SFMW847	01
Drowning In Berlin	Mobiles	SFMW831	04
Dub Be Good To Me	Beats International	SFMW852	10
Dude (Looks Like A Lady)	Aerosmith	SFMW862	07
Eastbound And Down	Jerry Reed	SFMW929	11
Easy Lover	Phil Collins And Phil Bailey	SFMW828	04
Ebay	Weird Al Yankovic	SFMW900	15
Eberneezer Goode	Shamen	SFMW831	08
Ebony And Ivory	Paul Mccartney And Stevie Won	SFMW916	14
Echo Beach	Martha-and-the Muffins	SFMW928	05
Edge Of Heaven	Wham	SFMW921	11
Ego	Saturdays	SFMW920	12
Eighth Day	Hazel O'connor	SFMW882	07
Einstein A Go Go	Landscape	SFMW845	06
El Manana	Gorillaz	SFMW879	12
El Salvador	Athlete	SFMW908	11
Eleanor Rigby	Beatles	SFMW842	09
Electric Avenue	Eddy Grant	SFMW805	04
Electric Feel	Mgmt	SFMW905	13
Eloise	Barry Ryan	SFMW900	04
Email My Heart	Britney Spears	SFMW815	12

Title	Artist	Code	#
Embraceable You	Frank Sinatra	SFMW915	12
Emma	Hot Chocolate	SFMW808	15
End Of The Line	Traveling Wilberys	SFMW851	07
End Of The Road	Boyz 2 Men	SFMW853	08
End Of The World	Susan Boyle	SFMW922	10
England 2 Columbia 0	Kirsty Maccoll	SFMW878	07
Enjoy The Silence	Depeche Mode	SFMW862	06
Enter Sandman	Metallica	SFMW852	11
Epiphany	Staind	SFMW841	10
Erotica	Madonna	SFMW824	01
Escape (The Pina Colada Song)	Rupert Holmes	SFMW837	03
Especially For You	Kylie Minogue And Jason Donov	SFMW804	05
Even Better Than The Real Thing	U2	SFMW850	07
Even Flow	Pearl Jam	SFMW901	01
Everlong	Foo Fighters	SFMW893	02
Every Day Hurts	Sad Cafe	SFMW875	14
Every Kind Of People	Robert Palmer	SFMW845	03
Every Little Thing She Does Is Magi	Police	SFMW812	05
Every Man Must Have A Dream	Liverpool Express	SFMW884	03
Every Rose Has It's Thorn	Poison	SFMW808	12
Everybody Loves Somebody	Dean Martin	SFMW887	15

Title	Artist	Code	Track
Everybody's Got To Learn Sometime	Korgis	SFMW871	15
Everybody's Makin' It Big But Me	Dr Hook	SFMW853	14
Everybody's Somebody's Fool	Connie Francis	SFMW879	13
Everybody's Talkin'	Harry Nilsson	SFMW818	06
Everyday	High School Musical 2	SFMW929	14
Everyday I Love You Less And Less	Kaiser Chiefs	SFMW865	12
Everyday I Think Of Money	Stereophonics	SFMW826	05
Everyday Is Like Sunday	Morrissey	SFMW870	08
Everyone Nose (All The Girls Standi	N E R D	SFMW906	06
Everything	Alanis Morissette	SFMW852	15
Everything	Michael Buble	SFMW899	04
Everything She Wants	Wham	SFMW920	16
Everytime We Touch	Cascada	SFMW924	07
Evil That Men Do	Iron Maiden	SFMW888	01
Express Yourself	Madonna	SFMW875	05
Express Yourself	Madonna	SFMW885	15
Fade To Grey	Visage	SFMW832	15
Faint	Linkin Park	SFMW853	10
Fairground	Simply Red	SFMW802	05
Fall To Pieces	Velvet Revolver	SFMW866	09
Falling	Julee Cruise	SFMW911	12
Family Affair	Mary J Blige	SFMW824	09

Title	Artist	Code
Family Man	Roachford	SFMW912 05
Fantasy Island	Tight Fit	SFMW831 05
Farewell My Summer Love	Michael Jackson	SFMW914 11
Fashion	David Bowie	SFMW820 14
Fast Car	Tracy Chapman	SFMW847 12
Fat Bottomed Girls	Queen	SFMW907 15
February Song	Josh Groban	SFMW901 13
Feed My Frankenstein	Alice Cooper	SFMW893 09
Feelin' Fine	Ultrabeat	SFMW870 10
Feeling Good	Nina Simone	SFMW900 07
Feelings	Morris Albert	SFMW901 10
Feels Like Heaven	Fiction Factory	SFMW825 02
Feels Like I'm In Love	Kelly Marie	SFMW802 14
Feilds Of Gold	Sting	SFMW806 02
Female Of The Species	Space	SFMW856 14
Fergus Sings The Blues	Deacon Blue	SFMW821 07
Ferry 'cross The Mersey	Gerry And The Pacemakers	SFMW857 14
Fever	Peggy Lee	SFMW841 01
Fever	Starsailor	SFMW841 06
Fields Of Gold	Eva Cassidy	SFMW855 02
Fight For Your Right To Party	Beastie Boys	SFMW852 07

Title	Artist	Code	Track
Find My Love	Fairground Attraction	SFMW844	15
Find Your Love	Drake	SFMW930	09
Finest	S O S Band	SFMW842	06
Fireball	Deep Purple	SFMW904	15
First Cut Is The Deepest	Sheryl Crow	SFMW852	01
First Time	Robin Beck	SFMW851	06
Fixer	Pearl Jam	SFMW917	12
Flashback	Imagination	SFMW844	05
Flashdance	Deep Dish	SFMW859	07
Flathead	Fratellis	SFMW887	06
Flood	Katie Melua	SFMW927	06
Floral Dance	Terry Wogan	SFMW895	07
Flowers	S W F	SFMW802	03
Fly Me To The Moon (In Other Words)	Tony Bennett	SFMW925	12
Flying	Bryan Adams	SFMW859	02
Follow You Follow Me	Genesis	SFMW844	06
Folsom Prison Blues	Johnny Cash	SFMW879	14
Fooled Around And Fell In Love	Elvin Bishop	SFMW898	07
Footprints In The Sand	Leona Lewis	SFMW912	12
Footsteps	Daniel O'donnell	SFMW859	08
For America	Red Box	SFMW885	08
For Those About To Rock	Ac Dc	SFMW817	04

Title	Artist	Code	
For Your Babies	Simply Red	SFMW806	10
For Your Love	Yardbirds	SFMW925	04
Forca	Nelly Furtado	SFMW856	12
Forever	Damage	SFMW850	13
Forever Live And Die	Omd	SFMW914	04
Forever Young	Bob Dylan	SFMW838	06
Forty Shades Of Green	Daniel O'donnell	SFMW851	12
Four Letter Word	Kim Wilde	SFMW869	10
Four Seasons In One Day	Crowded House	SFMW881	04
Four To The Floor	Starsailor	SFMW854	06
Foxy Lady	Jimi Hendrix Experience	SFMW872	03
Fred Astaire	James	SFMW858	09
Free Bird	Lynyrd Skynyrd	SFMW928	02
Free Electric Band	Albert Hammond	SFMW866	13
Free Fallin'	Tom Petty	SFMW871	08
Free Loop	Daniel Powter	SFMW872	14
Free Your Mind	En Vogue	SFMW834	04
Freedom	Wham	SFMW846	14
Freedom Come Freedom Go	Fortunes	SFMW822	13
Frog Chorus	Paul Mccartney	SFMW826	06
From Russia With Love	Matt Monro	SFMW885	13

Title	Artist	Code	Track
Frontin	Jamie Cullum	SFMW852	08
Full Of Grace	Sarah Mclachlan	SFMW844	07
Fun Fun Fun	Beach Boys	SFMW859	13
Funky Gibbon	Goodies	SFMW825	03
Funny Familiar Forgotten Feeling	Tom Jones	SFMW823	03
Future's So Bright I Gotta Wear Sha	Timbuk 3	SFMW903	13
Galway Girl	Mundy	SFMW915	14
Games People Play	Joe South	SFMW821	13
Games Without Frontiers	Peter Gabriel	SFMW865	02
Gang Bang	Black Lace	SFMW834	05
Gentle On My Mind	Glen Campbell	SFMW886	02
Georgy Girl	Seekers	SFMW894	05
Gertcha	Chas And Dave	SFMW874	10
Get Another Boyfriend	Backstreet Boys	SFMW843	02
Get Down Get With It	Slade	SFMW913	09
Get Here	Oleta Adams	SFMW850	08
Get Me Outta Here	Jet	SFMW860	04
Get On Your Feet	Gloria Estefan	SFMW876	08
Get Out Of Your Lazy Bed	Matt Bianco	SFMW831	06
Get Ready	Temptations	SFMW916	07
Get The Message	Electronic	SFMW884	12
Get The Phunk Out	Extreme	SFMW879	01

Title	Artist	Code	#
Get Up Offa That Thing	James Brown	SFMW896	04
Get Up Stand Up	Bob Marley	SFMW828	05
Getting Away With It	Electronic	SFMW893	14
Ghost Riders In The Sky	Vaughn Monroe	SFMW812	04
Ghost Town	Specials	SFMW806	14
Gilly Gill Ossenfeffer	Max Bygraves	SFMW846	04
Girl Can't Help It	Little Richard	SFMW931	06
Girl Is Mine	Paul Mccartney And M Jackson	SFMW829	12
Girl You Know It's True	Milli Vanilli	SFMW814	03
Girlfriend	Darkness	SFMW876	05
Girls Girls Girls	Sailor	SFMW863	09
Give A Little Bit	Supertramp	SFMW875	11
Give A Little Love	Bay City Rollers	SFMW822	05
Give It Away	Deepest Blue	SFMW851	08
Give Me Back My Heart	Dollar	SFMW909	09
Give Me Love	George Harrison	SFMW825	04
Give Me Strength	Burt Bacharack And Elvis Cost	SFMW819	12
Giving It All Away	Roger Daltrey	SFMW873	13
Glitter In The Air	Pink	SFMW924	05
Gloomy Sunday	Billie Holiday	SFMW914	06
Glory Of Love	Peter Cetera	SFMW806	09

Title	Artist	Code	No.
Go West	Pet Shop Boys	SFMW811	04
God And Satan	Biffy Clyro	SFMW929	02
God Gave Rock And Roll To You	Kiss	SFMW816	01
God Only Knows	Beach Boys	SFMW855	09
Goin' Out West	Tom Waits	SFMW867	10
Going Back To My Roots	Odyssey	SFMW911	04
Going Down	Mary J Blige	SFMW858	10
Going Down To Liverpool	Bangles	SFMW902	11
Going Through The Motions	Sarah Michelle Gellar	SFMW887	01
Going Under	Evanescence	SFMW897	04
Gold Digger	Glee Cast	SFMW923	15
Golden Touch	Razerlight	SFMW874	03
Golden Years	David Bowie	SFMW859	10
Good Luck	Basement Jaxx	SFMW857	10
Good People	Jack Johnson	SFMW875	01
Good Thing	Fine Young Cannibals	SFMW864	09
Good Tradition	Tanita Tikaram	SFMW862	04
Good Vibrations	Beach Boys	SFMW830	04
Goodbye Horses	Q Lazarus	SFMW917	06
Goodies Theme	Goodies	SFMW826	07
Got To Be Real	Cheryl Lynn	SFMW827	06
Got To Give It Up	Marvin Gaye	SFMW881	13

Title	Artist	Code
Grace	Jeff Buckley	SFMW859 06
Gravity	Embrace	SFMW859 01
Grease Megamix	Grease	SFMW881 15
Great Gig In The Sky	Pink Floyd	SFMW912 15
Great Pretender	Platters	SFMW924 12
Green Door	Shakin' Stevens	SFMW834 06
Groove Is In The Heart	Dee Lite	SFMW806 01
Groovy Kind Of Love	Phil Collins	SFMW888 14
Growing On Me	Darkness	SFMW847 15
Guantanamera	Trini Lopez	SFMW901 07
Guns And Horses	Ellie Goulding	SFMW927 08
Guns Of Brixton	Clash	SFMW909 01
H A P P Y Radio	Edwin Starr	SFMW916 05
Haitian Divorce	Steely Dan	SFMW859 03
Hakuna Matata	Lion King	SFMW871 07
Hallelujah	Rufus Wainwright	SFMW845 02
Halo Walking On Sunshine	Glee Cast	SFMW922 15
Handle With Care	Travelling Wilburys	SFMW876 14
Hands To Heaven	Breathe	SFMW888 08
Hanging By A Moment	Lifehouse	SFMW862 11
Hanging On The Telephone	Blondie	SFMW853 05

Title	Artist	Code	
Hanky Panky	Madonna	SFMW892	15
Happiness	Ken Dodd	SFMW821	14
Happy Birthday Sweet Sixteen	Neil Sedaka	SFMW814	14
Happy Happy Birthday Babe	Tune Weavers	SFMW877	12
Happy Hour	House Martins	SFMW830	05
Happy Talk	Captain Sensible	SFMW817	05
Hard Rain's Gonna Fall	Bryan Ferry	SFMW902	02
Hard To Beat	Hard-fi	SFMW923	03
Hard To Say I'm Sorry	Peter Cetera	SFMW808	14
Harden My Heart	Quarterflash	SFMW902	10
Harder I Try	Brother Beyond	SFMW911	11
Harder To Breathe	Maroon 5	SFMW855	05
Hasta Manana	Abba	SFMW929	05
Have A Cigar	Pink Floyd	SFMW911	01
He Could Be The One	Hannah Montana	SFMW928	14
He Was Really Saying Somethin'	Velvelettes	SFMW918	14
Head Like A Hole	Nine Inch Nails	SFMW898	04
Head Over Heels	Tears For Fears	SFMW850	11
Heading For The Light	Traveling Wilburys	SFMW911	15
Heal The Pain	George Michael	SFMW826	08
Heart Shaped Box	Nirvana	SFMW896	02
Heartache Avenue	Maisonettes	SFMW874	11

Title	Artist	Code	
Heartache Tonight	Michael Buble	SFMW923	13
Heartbeat	Enrique Iglesias-feat -nichol	SFMW929	03
Hearts On Fire	John Cafferty	SFMW877	03
Heat Is On	Glenn Frey	SFMW803	15
Heatseeker	Ac Dc	SFMW882	13
Heaven	Bryan Adams	SFMW883	09
Heaven (Slow Version)	Dj Sammy	SFMW837	10
Heaven Can Wait	Meat Loaf	SFMW876	15
Heaven Help	Lenny Kravitz	SFMW825	14
Heaven In Your Eyes	Loverboy	SFMW912	06
Heaven Knows I'm Miserable Now	Smiths	SFMW853	07
Heaven Must Have Sent You	Elgins	SFMW817	12
Helen Wheels	Paul Mccartney	SFMW906	15
Hello Again	Neil Diamond	SFMW835	12
Hello This Is Joannie	Paul Evans	SFMW913	03
Hello World	Lady Antebellum	SFMW932	14
Hells Bells	Ac Dc	SFMW863	08
Help Me Make It Through The Night	John Holt	SFMW866	05
Here And Now	Del Amitri	SFMW895	04
Here Comes The Rain Again	Eurythmics	SFMW830	06
Here Comes The Sun	Beatles	SFMW872	05

Title	Artist	Code	Track
Here Comes The Sun	Steve Harley	SFMW834	07
Here We Go	Stakka Bo	SFMW879	05
Here You Come Again	Dolly Parton	SFMW822	04
Here's Where The Story Ends	Sundays	SFMW905	08
Hero Takes A Fall	Bangles	SFMW896	12
Hersham Boys	Sham 69	SFMW890	05
He's On The Phone	St Etienne	SFMW884	11
Hey Dj I Can't Dance To That Music	Beatmasters And Betty Boo	SFMW893	07
Hey Girl Don't Bother Me	Tams	SFMW813	07
Hey Good Lookin	Hank Williams	SFMW821	10
Hey Hey We're The Monkees	Monkees	SFMW826	09
Hey Paula	Paul And Paula	SFMW805	02
Hey Soul Sister	Train	SFMW927	04
Hey Stoopid	Alice Cooper	SFMW897	13
Hey There Lonely Girl	Eddie Holman	SFMW816	04
Hey Ya	Outkast	SFMW849	01
Hey You	Bachman-turner Overdrive	SFMW901	03
Hi Fidelity	Kids From Fame	SFMW841	04
Hi Heel Sneekers	Cross Section	SFMW878	04
Hi Hi Hi	Paul Mccartney	SFMW900	01
Higher Than A Hawk (Deeper Than A W	Howard Keel	SFMW908	14
Hip To Be Square	Huey Lewis And The News	SFMW805	14

Title	Artist	Code
Hiphopapotamus Vs Rhymenocerous	Flight Of The Conchords	SFMW908 16
Hippy Chick	Soho	SFMW877 06
History In The Making	Darius Rucker	SFMW926 13
History Repeating	Shirley Bassey And The Propel	SFMW869 15
Hit Me With Your Best Shot	Pat Benatar	SFMW899 02
Hold My Hand	Hootie And The Blowfish	SFMW881 05
Hold On	Wilson Phillips	SFMW872 10
Hold On Tight	Electric Light Orchestra	SFMW885 01
Hollywood	Marina And The Diamonds	SFMW922 05
Honest Mistake	Bravery	SFMW864 05
Honey I'm Home	Shania Twain	SFMW815 02
Honeybee	Gloria Gaynor	SFMW910 08
Hot Fudge	Robbie Williams	SFMW863 04
Hot In Here	Nelly	SFMW848 07
Hot In The City	Billy Idol	SFMW814 11
Hot Water	Level 42	SFMW921 15
Hounds Of Love	Kate Bush	SFMW868 10
House Is Not A Home	Brook Benton	SFMW819 01
House Of Love	East 17	SFMW849 08
House That Jack Built	Tracie Young	SFMW912 07
How Blue Can You Get	B B King	SFMW894 08

Title	Artist	Code	#
How Come	Ronnie Lane	SFMW928	10
How Come How Long	Babyface-feat -stevie Wonder	SFMW932	06
How Do You Like Your Eggs In The Mo	Dean Martin And H O'connell	SFMW870	03
Human Touch	Bruce Springsteen	SFMW836	06
Human Touch	Rick Springfield	SFMW900	03
Hunger Strike	Temple Of The Dog	SFMW913	12
Hungry Like The Wolf	Duran Duran	SFMW816	10
Hunting High And Low	A Ha	SFMW820	15
Hurt	Johnny Cash	SFMW891	15
Hymn	Ultravox	SFMW914	14
Hymn To Her	Pretenders	SFMW865	10
I Am A Man Of Constant Sorrow	Soggy Bottom Boys	SFMW908	15
I Am A Real American	Rick Derringer	SFMW917	14
I Am Not A Robot	Marina And The Diamonds	SFMW927	10
I Am The Beat	Look	SFMW878	02
I Am What I Am	Gloria Gaynor	SFMW804	07
I Believe	Fantasia	SFMW856	11
I Believe I Can Fly	R Kelly	SFMW861	03
I Believe In You And Me	Whitney Houston	SFMW813	11
I Bet You Look Good On The Danceflo	Arctic Monkeys	SFMW871	01
I Can Hear Music	Beach Boys	SFMW824	12
I Can't Dance	Genesis	SFMW804	06

I Can't Get No Satisfaction	Rolling Stones	SFMW856 06
I Can't Let You Go	Ian Van Dahl	SFMW848 13
I Can't Stand Up (For Falling Down)	Elvis Costello	SFMW904 06
I Can't Stop	Osmonds	SFMW907 08
I Couldn't Live Without Your Love	Petula Clark	SFMW836 14
I Don't Believe You	Pink	SFMW919 10
I Don't Feel Like Dancin'	Baseballs	SFMW929 15
I Don't Wanna Dance	Eddy Grant	SFMW805 05
I Don't Wanna Fall In Love	Jane Childs	SFMW843 03
I Don't Want To Be Alone Tonight	Dr Hook	SFMW822 10
I Don't Want To Talk About It	Everything But The Girl	SFMW809 07
I Don't Want To Wait	Paula Cole	SFMW839 07
I Dreamed A Dream	Susan Boyle	SFMW917 11
I Fall To Pieces	Patsy Cline	SFMW812 10
I Feel Free	Cream	SFMW843 04
I Fought The Law	Clash	SFMW849 11
I Got 5 On It	Luniz	SFMW863 13
I Got You (I Feel Good)	James Brown	SFMW824 07
I Haven't Stopped Dancing Yet	Gonzalez	SFMW868 11
I Just Can't Help Believing	Elvis Presley	SFMW857 02
I Know Where It's At	All Saints	SFMW885 10

Title	Artist	Code	Track
I Like The Way	Bodyrockers	SFMW867	08
I Love It Loud	Kiss	SFMW879	06
I Love You	Sarah Mclachlan	SFMW897	05
I Love You More Than Rock And Roll	Thunder	SFMW898	15
I O U	Freeze	SFMW833	07
I Owe You Nothing	Bros	SFMW807	03
I Ran	Flock Of Seagulls	SFMW861	15
I Really Didn't Mean It	Luther Vandross	SFMW833	06
I Second That Emotion	Japan	SFMW831	07
I See Right Through You	Alanis Morissette	SFMW834	08
I Surrender	Rainbow	SFMW916	02
I Swear	All 4 One	SFMW916	13
I Swear	John Michael Montgomery	SFMW813	10
I Tried	Brandy	SFMW861	11
I Walk The Line	Johnny Cash	SFMW889	15
I Wanna Be Free	Elvis Presley	SFMW803	02
I Wanna Be Satisfied	Ramones	SFMW926	04
I Wanna Do Bad Things With You	Jace Everett	SFMW931	01
I Wanna Have Your Babies	Natasha Bedingfield	SFMW891	09
I Want To Be Free	Toyah	SFMW842	07
I Want To Be Wanted	Brenda Lee	SFMW878	15
I Want You	Inspiral Carpets	SFMW877	05

Title	Artist	Code	#
I Want You Back In My Life	Alice Deejay	SFMW838	12
I Wanted Everything	Ramones	SFMW910	02
I Will Be There	Britney Spears	SFMW815	11
I Wonder Why	Curtis Stigers	SFMW802	07
I Won't Back Down	Tom Petty	SFMW897	11
I Write Sins Not Tragedies	Panic At The Disco	SFMW886	09
Ice In The Sun	Status Quo	SFMW803	08
I'd Do It All Again	Corinne Bailey-rae	SFMW922	12
I'd Love You To Want Me	Lobo	SFMW807	11
I'd Rather Be With You	Joshua Radin	SFMW925	10
I'd Rather Jack	Reynolds Girls	SFMW891	05
If I Can Dream	Elvis Presley	SFMW837	13
If I Can't Change Your Mind	Sugar	SFMW912	02
If I Didn't Have A Dime	Gene Pitney	SFMW824	13
If I Die Young	Band Perry	SFMW931	12
If I Was	Midge Ure	SFMW812	06
If I Were A Rich Man	Topol	SFMW891	13
If It Makes You Happy	Sheryl Crow	SFMW812	09
If She Knew What She Wants	Bangles	SFMW887	08
If The Kids Are United	Sham 69	SFMW892	02
If This Is It	Huey Lewis And The News	SFMW814	06

Title	Artist	Code
If You Can't Give Me Love	Suzi Quatro	SFMW822 03
If You Love Me	Brenda Lee	SFMW816 03
If You Only Knew	Shinedown	SFMW922 01
If You Were Here Tonight	Alexander O'neal	SFMW845 12
If You're Wondering If I Want You T	Weezer	SFMW921 03
I'll Be There	Jackson 5	SFMW917 09
I'll Be Your Baby Tonight	U B 40	SFMW807 10
I'll Never Be Maria Magdalena	Sandra	SFMW922 04
I'll Never Fall In Love Again	Deacon Blue	SFMW864 08
I'll Never Fall In Love Again	Dion Warwick	SFMW874 15
I'll Pick A Rose For My Rose	Mary Johnson	SFMW817 13
I'll Say Forever My Love	Jimmy Ruffin	SFMW818 14
I'll Take A Melody	John Holt	SFMW848 05
I'm Always Here (Baywatch Theme)	Jimi Jameson	SFMW920 09
I'm Doing Fine Now	Pasadenas	SFMW806 15
I'm Not Crying	Flight Of The Conchords	SFMW915 15
I'm Not Okay	My Chemical Romance	SFMW867 06
I'm On My Way	Dean Parrish	SFMW921 06
I'm On My Way	Proclaimers	SFMW824 14
I'm Only Sleeping	Beatles	SFMW899 11
I'm Sticking With You	Velvet Underground	SFMW903 10
I'm Still Standing	Elton John	SFMW823 12

Title	Artist	Code	#
I'm The One	Who	SFMW902	14
I'm Through With Love	Marilyn Monroe	SFMW904	11
I'm Waiting For The Man	Velvet Underground	SFMW854	13
Impossible Dream	Jack Jones	SFMW836	13
In A Broken Dream	Python Lee Jackson	SFMW872	09
In All The Right Places	Lisa Stansfield	SFMW848	08
In Between Days	Cure	SFMW915	08
In My Life	Beatles	SFMW839	05
In Over My Head	Dr Hook	SFMW858	11
In The City	Jam	SFMW906	04
In The Heat Of The Night	Susanna	SFMW925	07
In The Meantime	Spacehog	SFMW912	14
In The Name Of The Father	Black Grape	SFMW898	12
In The Shadows	Rasmus	SFMW851	01
In The Still Of The Night	Five Satins	SFMW821	09
In These Shoes	Kirsty Mccall	SFMW870	13
In Too Deep	Genesis	SFMW827	10
In Your Eyes	George Benson	SFMW820	01
In Your Room	Bangles	SFMW893	04
Inbetweener	Sleeper	SFMW894	06
Incommunicado	Marillion	SFMW897	15

Title	Artist	Code	#
Infected	The The	SFMW880	03
Inhale	Stone Sour	SFMW843	05
Innuendo	Queen	SFMW807	04
Into The Great Wide Open	Tom Petty And The Heartbreake	SFMW907	02
Into Your Arms	Lemonheads	SFMW915	10
Iris	Goo Goo Dolls	SFMW846	02
Irish Blood English Heart	Morrissey	SFMW852	05
Iron Fist	Iron Maiden	SFMW892	04
Iron Man	Black Sabbath	SFMW926	01
Ironic	Alanis Morissette	SFMW809	13
Is She Really Going Out With Him	Joe Jackson	SFMW821	12
Is This Love	Bob Marley	SFMW834	10
Is This The Way Life's Meant To Be	Electric Light Orchestra	SFMW906	14
Is Vic There	Department S	SFMW905	14
Isn't It A Pity	George Harrison	SFMW904	05
It Ain't Easy	David Bowie	SFMW838	03
It Doesn't Matter	Alison Krauss	SFMW890	07
It Don't Come Easy	Ringo Starr	SFMW818	07
It Had To Be You	Harry Connick Jnr	SFMW826	10
It's A Heartache	Bonnie Tyler	SFMW804	12
It's A Long Way To The Top	Ac Dc	SFMW879	03
It's A Man's Man's World	James Brown	SFMW807	08

Title	Artist	Code	
It's A Miracle	Barry Manilow	SFMW836	02
It's A Sin	Pet Shop Boys	SFMW807	01
It's All Over Now	Rolling Stones	SFMW813	14
It's All Over Now Baby Blue	Bob Dylan	SFMW869	03
It's Alright Baby's Coming Back	Eurythmics	SFMW896	09
It's Been A While	Staind	SFMW845	08
It's Been So Long	George Mccr'	SFMW802	15
It's Beginning To Look A Lot Like C	Dean Martin	SFMW918	17
It's Five O'clock Somewhere	Alan Jackson And Jimmy Buffet	SFMW854	11
It's Gonna Be A Cold Cold Christmas	Dana	SFMW918	18
It's My Life	Talk Talk	SFMW904	03
It's Probaly Me	Sting	SFMW839	13
It's Raining	Darts	SFMW907	06
I've Got A Woman	Ray Charles	SFMW932	11
Jack And Diane	John Cougar Mellencamp	SFMW862	01
Jack O' Diamonds	Lonnie Donegan	SFMW887	09
Jackson	Nancy Sinatra And Lee Hazelwo	SFMW929	10
Jailbait	Motorhead	SFMW869	14
Jailbreak	Thin Lizzy	SFMW863	11
Jammin'	Bob Marley	SFMW805	09
Je T'aime (Moi Non Plus)	Serge Gainsbourg And Jane Bir	SFMW900	06

Title	Artist	Code	#
Jeans On	David Dundas	SFMW822	12
Jeremy	Pearl Jam	SFMW854	14
Jessie's Girl	Rick Springfield	SFMW873	10
Jesus He Knows You	Genesis	SFMW839	11
Jesus Of Suburbia	Green Day	SFMW873	06
Jesus Take The Wheel	Carrie Underwood	SFMW890	12
Jezebel	Frankie Laine	SFMW863	03
Jive Talkin'	Bee Gees	SFMW929	06
Joanna	Scott Walker	SFMW817	15
Joe Le Taxi	Vannessa Paradis	SFMW825	05
Johnny B Goode	Chuck Berry	SFMW862	02
Johnny Come Home	Fine Young Cannibals	SFMW871	02
Joshua	Dolly Parton	SFMW885	12
Joyride	Roxette	SFMW808	11
Juicebox	Strokes	SFMW873	02
Julia	Chris Rea	SFMW918	15
Julie Do You Love Me	White Plains	SFMW813	03
Jump Around	House Of Pain	SFMW850	02
Jump In Line (Shake Shake)	Beetlejuice	SFMW837	12
Jump Then Fall	Taylor Swift	SFMW919	06
Jumpin' Jack Flash	Rolling Stones	SFMW870	12
Jungle Love	Time	SFMW895	03

Title	Artist	Code	Track
Just Be Good To Me	S O S Band	SFMW839	03
Just Breathe	Pearl Jam	SFMW922	02
Just Like A Woman	Nina Simone	SFMW931	09
Just One Look	Doris Troy	SFMW824	05
Just The One	Levellers	SFMW881	10
Just The Way You Are	Barry White	SFMW812	07
Just What I Always Wanted	Mari Wilson	SFMW899	14
Karmacoma	Massive Attack	SFMW892	07
Keep Holding On	Avril Lavigne	SFMW886	15
Keep It Dark	Genesis	SFMW897	02
Keep Your Hands Off My Girl	Good Charlotte	SFMW886	13
Keeping The Dream Alive	Freiheit	SFMW930	16
Kelly	Del Shannon	SFMW864	15
Kick In The Eye	Bauhaus	SFMW840	14
Kick Push	Lupe Fiasco	SFMW879	08
Kickstarts	Example	SFMW927	14
Kids With Guns	Gorillaz	SFMW877	02
Killer	Adamski	SFMW844	08
Killing Moon	Echo And The Bunnyman	SFMW851	10
Killing Moon (Original Version)	Echo And The Bunnymen	SFMW854	10
King Of Emotion	Big Country	SFMW888	03

Title	Artist	Code
King Of Rock And Roll	Prefab Sprout	SFMW825 12
Kings And Queens	30 Seconds To Mars	SFMW920 07
Kinky Boots	Patrick Mcknee And Honour Bla	SFMW848 14
Kiss Me	Stephen Tintin Duffy	SFMW884 06
Kiss Me Honey Honey Kiss Me	Shirley Bassey	SFMW835 13
Kiss On My List	Hall And Oates	SFMW918 11
Kiss This Thing Goodbye	Del Amitri	SFMW837 07
Kiss With A Fist	Florence And The Machine	SFMW907 12
Knicker Elastic King	Rutles	SFMW911 13
Knock On Wood	Ami Stewart	SFMW827 07
Krafty	New Order	SFMW864 07
Kyrie	Mr Mister	SFMW833 08
L S I	Shamen	SFMW883 06
La Vie En Rose	Edith Piaf	SFMW901 08
Labour Of Love	Hue And Cry	SFMW835 15
Ladies Of The World	Flight Of The Conchords	SFMW909 15
Lady	Commodores	SFMW833 12
Lady Madonna	Beatles	SFMW801 01
Land Of Make Believe	Bucks Fizz	SFMW818 02
Last Goodbye	Jeff Buckley	SFMW866 02
Last Kiss	David Cassidy	SFMW838 09
Last Name	Carrie Underwood	SFMW926 10

Title	Artist	Code	
Last Night	Strokes	SFMW835	09
Last Night A Dj Saved My Life	Indeep	SFMW838	11
Last Night At Danceland	Randy Crawford	SFMW918	09
Last Request	Paolo Nutini	SFMW878	06
Last Time	Rolling Stones	SFMW802	09
Last Train Home	Lost Prophets	SFMW870	11
Lately	Stevie Wonder	SFMW826	11
Laughing Policeman	Charles Penrose	SFMW905	05
Laughter In The Rain	Neil Sedaka	SFMW814	13
Laura	Scissor Sisters	SFMW855	01
Lavender	Marillion	SFMW898	01
Leah	Roy Orbison	SFMW873	11
Lean On Me	Red Box	SFMW883	02
Learn To Fly	Foo Fighters	SFMW833	09
Learning To Fly	Tom Petty And The Heartbreake	SFMW887	02
Leave A Light On	Belinda Carlisle	SFMW864	03
Leaving On A Jet Plane	John Denver	SFMW924	04
Leningrad	Billy Joel	SFMW855	11
Les Artistes	Santogold	SFMW901	12
Let It Be	Beatles	SFMW823	06
Let Me Be Your Fantasy	Baby D	SFMW817	08

Title	Artist	Code
Let Me Kiss You	Morrissey	SFMW857 09
Let The Music Play	Barry White	SFMW809 01
Let The River Run	Carly Simon	SFMW926 07
Let There Be Rock	Ac Dc	SFMW880 07
Let Your Loss Be Your Lesson	Robert Plant And Alison Kraus	SFMW911 09
Let's Dance To Joy Division	Wombats	SFMW894 14
Let's Get Ready To Rhumble	Pj And Duncan	SFMW831 09
Let's Get Rocked	Def Leppard	SFMW885 07
Let's Go Surfing	Drums	SFMW928 04
Let's Hear It For The Boy	Denise Williams	SFMW831 10
Liberian Girl	Michael Jackson	SFMW914 16
Licence To Kill	Gladys Knight	SFMW845 01
Lick It Up	Kiss	SFMW881 03
Life Is A Lemon And I Want My Mone	Meat Loaf	SFMW882 09
Life Is Life	Opus	SFMW838 15
Life Of Illusion	Joe Walsh	SFMW905 03
Life's What You Make It	Talk Talk	SFMW859 11
Lift Me Up	Yes	SFMW901 15
Light Me Up	Pretty Reckless	SFMW929 13
Like A Rolling Stone	Bob Dylan	SFMW924 11
Like To Get To Know You Well	Howard Jones	SFMW832 05
Lips Like Sugar	Echo And The Bunnymen	SFMW921 04

Title	Artist	Code
Lipstick On Your Collar	Connie Francis	SFMW866 10
Listen Like Thieves	Inxs	SFMW869 08
Listen To What The Man Said	Wings	SFMW823 01
Lithium	Evanescence	SFMW886 14
Little Bit Of Snow	Howard Jones	SFMW826 01
Little Drummer Boy	Jessica Simpson And Ashlee Si	SFMW858 08
Little Green Bag	George Baker Collection	SFMW872 15
Little More Love	Olivia Newton John	SFMW879 15
Little Red Corvette	Prince	SFMW846 09
Little Respect	Erasure	SFMW807 09
Little White Bull	Tommy Steele	SFMW820 13
Live It Up	Mental As Anything	SFMW860 12
Live Like You Were Dying	Tim Mcgraw	SFMW853 15
Live To Tell	Madonna	SFMW824 02
Live Your Life Be Free	Belinda Carlisle	SFMW903 06
Livin' On A Prayer	Bon Jovi	SFMW838 04
Living After Midnight	Judas Priest	SFMW893 15
Living In A Box	Living In A Box	SFMW891 03
Living It Up	Level 42	SFMW865 04
Living On My Own	Freddie Mercury	SFMW804 04
Loads A Money	Harry Enfield	SFMW830 07

Title	Artist	Code
Loco	Fun Loving Criminals	SFMW896 05
Loco In Acapulco	Four Tops	SFMW863 14
Locomotion	Omd	SFMW873 08
Logical Song	Supertramp	SFMW873 04
Lollipop	Chordettes	SFMW915 09
London Bridge	Fergie	SFMW885 05
London Calling	Clash	SFMW806 03
London Nights	London Boys	SFMW812 02
Loneliness Knows Me By Name	Westlife	SFMW815 14
Lonely Goatherd	Julie Andrews	SFMW908 08
Lonely Teardrops	Huey Lewis	SFMW866 04
Lonely This Christmas	Mick Jagger And Joss Stone	SFMW857 04
Long And Winding Road	Beatles	SFMW823 09
Long Hot Summer	Style Council	SFMW832 14
Long Run	Eagles	SFMW926 02
Longview	Green Day	SFMW918 01
Look	Roxette	SFMW811 03
Look Of Love	Dusty Springfield	SFMW819 02
Look What They've Done To My Song	New Seekers	SFMW827 01
Looking For Water	Alex Parks	SFMW872 12
Losing You	Dusty Springfield	SFMW889 12
Lost Weekend	Lloyd Cole And The Commotions	SFMW837 02

Title	Artist	Code
Louie Louie	Kingsmen	SFMW895 05
Love And Affection	Joan Armatrading	SFMW903 11
Love And Anger	Kate Bush	SFMW913 04
Love Boat	Jack Jones	SFMW894 10
Love Can't Turn Around	Farley Jackmaster Funk	SFMW903 05
Love Cats	Cure	SFMW808 08
Love Hurts	Nazareth	SFMW866 06
Love In An Elevator	Aerosmith	SFMW805 12
Love Insurrection	Alison Moyet	SFMW814 09
Love Is A Battlefield	Chapman And Knight	SFMW863 05
Love Is A Battlefield	Pat Benatar	SFMW875 04
Love Is Like A Butterfly	Dolly Parton	SFMW904 08
Love Is The Drug	Roxy Music	SFMW853 03
Love Is The Law	Seahorses	SFMW887 12
Love Letter	Bonnie Raitt	SFMW919 11
Love Letters	Alison Moyet	SFMW820 10
Love Me Do	Beatles	SFMW823 08
Love Me Like That	Michelle Branch and Sheryl Cr	SFMW931 07
Love Of My Life	Queen	SFMW921 09
Love On Your Side	Thompson Twins	SFMW830 08
Love Rears It's Ugly Head	Living Color	SFMW825 13

Title	Artist	Code
Love So Beautiful	Roy Orbison	SFMW837 04
Love Song	Simple Minds	SFMW916 01
Love The One You're With	Crosby Stills Nash And Young	SFMW924 03
Love Unemotional	Richard Marx	SFMW830 09
Love Walked In	Thunder	SFMW882 06
Love Will Keep Us Alive	Eagles	SFMW876 02
Love Will Save The Day	Whitney Houston	SFMW824 04
Love Will Tear Us Apart	Joy Division	SFMW825 06
Love You More	Sunscreem	SFMW903 02
Lovely Rita	Beatles	SFMW875 08
Loverboy	Dirty Dancing	SFMW837 11
Lover's Holiday	Change	SFMW874 08
Love's Been Good To Me	Frank Sinatra	SFMW882 17
Loves Got A Hold Of Me	Dollar	SFMW813 08
Love's Great Adventure	Ultravox	SFMW906 10
Low Life In High Places	Thunder	SFMW890 06
Lucrecia My Reflection	Sisters Of Mercy	SFMW891 07
Lucy In The Sky With Diamonds	Elton John	SFMW827 15
Luka	Suzanne Vega	SFMW811 12
Lullaby	Cure	SFMW912 03
Lump	Presidents Of The Usa	SFMW894 07
Lying In The Arms Of Mary	Sutherland Bros	SFMW805 06

Title	Artist	Code
Ma Baker	Boney M	SFMW829 07
Ma He's Making Eyes At Me	Lena Zavarone	SFMW843 06
Ma Ma Ma Belle	Electric Light Orchestra	SFMW896 15
Mad About The Boy	Dinah Washington	SFMW910 10
Mad World	Tears For Fears	SFMW831 11
Madame Helga	Stereophonics	SFMW838 10
Mainstreet	Bob Seger And The Silver Bull	SFMW923 09
Major-general's Song	Pirates Of Penzance	SFMW899 06
Make It Easy On Yourself	Jackie Trent	SFMW819 05
Make Me An Island	Joe Dolan	SFMW858 07
Make Me Wanna Die	Pretty Reckless	SFMW928 13
Make Someone Happy	Jimmy Durante	SFMW911 07
Making Plans For Nigel	X T C	SFMW841 07
Male Stripper	Man 2 Man Meets Man Parish	SFMW891 08
Mama	Genesis	SFMW828 06
Man For All Seasons	Robbie Williams	SFMW841 02
Man In The Mirror	Michael Jackson	SFMW838 13
Man Who Sold The World	David Bowie	SFMW897 01
Man With The Child In His Eyes	Kate Bush	SFMW895 15
Man Without Love	Engelbert Humperdink	SFMW856 13
Manchild	Neneh Cherry	SFMW881 09

Title	Artist	Code	Track
Mandy	Barry Manilow	SFMW920	11
Maneater	Daryl Hall And John Oates	SFMW809	02
Maniac	Michael Sembello	SFMW807	06
Many Of Horror	Biffy Clyro	SFMW931	15
Mardy Bum	Arctic Monkeys	SFMW921	07
Margaritaville	Jimmy Buffett	SFMW918	10
Maria	West Side Story	SFMW927	15
Maria Maria	Santana And The Product	SFMW805	10
Marlene On The Wall	Suzanne Vega	SFMW916	10
Marrakesh Express	Crosby Stills Nash And Young	SFMW855	07
Martha's Harbour	All About Eve	SFMW888	09
Mary's Prayer	Danny Wilson	SFMW924	01
Masterplan	Oasis	SFMW847	08
Matthew And Son	Cat Stevens	SFMW915	07
May It Be (Fellowship Of The Rings)	Enya	SFMW844	09
Maybe Tomorrow	Terry Bush	SFMW854	15
Mayhem	Imelda May	SFMW930	08
Me And Bobby Mcgee	Kris Kristofferson	SFMW851	04
Me And My Life	Tremeloes And Roberta Flack	SFMW803	07
Me And You Versus The World	Space	SFMW894	02
Mellow Yellow	Donovan	SFMW904	07
Men In Brown	Weird Al Yankovic	SFMW829	06

Title	Artist	Code
Mess Of Blues	Elvis Presley	SFMW803 04
Message	Grandmaster Flash	SFMW806 13
Metal Guru	T Rex	SFMW813 06
Middle	Jimmy Eat World	SFMW928 09
Midlife Crisis	Faith No More	SFMW894 15
Miles To Go	Celine Dion	SFMW841 11
Million Love Songs	Take That	SFMW815 07
Minnie The Moocher	Cab Calloway	SFMW812 01
Minor Variation	Billy Joel	SFMW826 12
Miracle Song	Neil Sedaka	SFMW880 14
Mirror In The Bathroom	Beat	SFMW867 04
Mirror Mirror	Dollar	SFMW829 14
Miss Independent	Kelly Clarkson	SFMW849 09
Miss You Like Crazy	Natalie Cole	SFMW808 13
Mist Mountain Hop	Led Zeppelin	SFMW839 09
Model	Kraftwerk	SFMW840 12
Modern Girl	Meat Loaf	SFMW904 02
Modern Love	David Bowie	SFMW924 06
Molly's Chambers	Kings Of Leon	SFMW868 13
Monday Monday	Mama's And Papa's	SFMW818 13
Money Don't Matter 2 Night	Prince	SFMW860 09

Title	Artist	Code
Money For Nothing	Dire Straits	SFMW865 06
Money's Too Tight	Simply Red	SFMW806 11
Monkey Gone To Heaven	Pixies	SFMW843 07
Monkey Wrench	Foo Fighters	SFMW882 01
Moondance	Van Morrison	SFMW838 05
Moonlight Shadow	Mike Oldfield	SFMW809 05
Moonlighting	Al Jarreau	SFMW834 09
Moonraker	Shirley Bassey	SFMW884 15
Moonshadow	Cat Stevens	SFMW905 04
More Like Her	Miranda Lambert	SFMW922 13
More Like The Movies	Dr Hook	SFMW822 09
More More More	Carmel	SFMW828 03
More Than A Feeling	Boston	SFMW920 08
More Than This	Roxy Music	SFMW809 04
More To Life	Stacey Orrico	SFMW847 05
Most Beautiful Girl	Flight Of The Conchords	SFMW910 15
Mother	Pink Floyd	SFMW841 12
Motherless Children	Eric Clapton	SFMW895 01
Motorcycle Emptiness	Manic Street Preachers	SFMW843 08
Mountains	Biffy Clyro	SFMW919 03
Move On	David Jordan	SFMW901 11
Move On Up	Curtis Mayfield	SFMW862 12

Title	Artist	Code	Track
Move Ya Body	Nina Sky	SFMW854	01
Movin' On Up	Primal Scream	SFMW915	06
Moving Out Today	Carol Bayer Sager	SFMW878	14
Mr Bojangles	John Holt	SFMW845	04
Mr Brightside	Killers	SFMW863	01
Mr Clean	Jam	SFMW908	06
Mr E's Beautiful Blues	Eels	SFMW923	07
Mr Jones	Counting Crows	SFMW833	10
Mr Rock And Roll	Amy Macdonald	SFMW899	07
Mr Sandman	Four Aces	SFMW880	09
Mr Telephone Man	New Edition	SFMW900	10
Mrs Robinson	Lemonheads	SFMW869	06
Munich	Editors	SFMW919	08
Murphy And The Bricks	Noel Murphy	SFMW902	13
My Aphrodisiac Is You	Katie Melua	SFMW859	04
My Best Friends Girl	Cars	SFMW808	09
My Blue Ridge Mountin Boy	Dolly Parton	SFMW886	06
My Boy Lollipop	Millie	SFMW814	02
My Brother	Terry Scott	SFMW907	09
My Camera Never Lies	Bucks Fizz	SFMW840	04
My Definition Of A Boombastic Jazz	Dream Warriors	SFMW893	13

Title	Artist	Code
My Favourite Game	Cardigans	SFMW855 15
My Favourite Things	Julie Andrews	SFMW907 16
My Generation	Who	SFMW855 13
My Give A Damn's Busted	Jo Dee Messina	SFMW891 12
My Grandfather's Clock	Standard	SFMW820 11
My Heart Belongs To Daddy	Marilyn Monroe	SFMW909 11
My Hero	Foo Fighters	SFMW892 03
My Humps	Black Eyed Peas	SFMW874 12
My Immortal	Evanescence	SFMW849 07
My Kz Ur Bf	Everything Everything	SFMW929 08
My Lovin' (You're Never Gonna Get I	En Vogue	SFMW833 11
My Name Is Not Susan	Whitney Houston	SFMW827 04
My Sister	Juliana Hatfield	SFMW915 11
My Town	Glass Tiger	SFMW907 01
Naive	Kooks	SFMW876 03
Nancy Boy	Placebo	SFMW885 04
Nearly Lost You	Screaming Trees	SFMW913 13
Needle In A Haystack	Velvelettes	SFMW916 09
Neighbourhood	Space	SFMW892 11
Neutron Star Collision (Love Is For	Muse	SFMW927 02
Never Before	Deep Purple	SFMW895 10
Never Can Say Goodbye	Gloria Gaynor	SFMW801 02

Title	Artist	Code
Never Can Say Goodbye	Jimmy Somerville	SFMW821 11
Never Ending Story	Limahl	SFMW811 15
Never Let Her Slip Away	Andrew Gold	SFMW808 05
Never Never	Assembly	SFMW925 08
Never Really Was	Mario Winans	SFMW856 15
Never Tear Us Apart	Inxs	SFMW860 03
Never Tear Us Apart	Tom Jones And Natalie Imbrugl	SFMW830 10
New England	Billy Bragg	SFMW861 08
New Rose	Damned	SFMW847 02
New Song	Howard Jones	SFMW830 11
New York	Paloma Faith	SFMW918 07
New York Minute	Don Henley	SFMW892 13
Nice And Sleazy	Stranglers	SFMW880 02
Nice One Cyril	Cockerel Chorus	SFMW818 08
Night	Frankie Valli	SFMW816 05
Night Owl	Gerry Rafferty	SFMW869 02
No Bravery	James Blunt	SFMW906 08
No Doubt About It	Hot Chocolate	SFMW825 07
No Easy Way Out	Robert Tepper	SFMW883 12
No Excuses	Alice In Chains	SFMW877 01
No More Heroes	Stranglers	SFMW886 04

Title	Artist	Code	#
No More Lonely Nights	Paul Mccartney	SFMW816	11
No One	Alicia Keys	SFMW896	13
No One Knows	Queens Of The Stone Age	SFMW866	14
No One Needs To Know	Shania Twain	SFMW836	10
No Son Of Mine	Genesis	SFMW865	11
No Woman No Cry	Bob Marley	SFMW856	03
Nobody Does It Better	Carly Simon	SFMW850	05
Nobody Needs Your Love	Gene Pitney	SFMW861	09
Nobody's Diary	Yazoo	SFMW826	13
Nobody's Fool	Avril Lavigne	SFMW855	06
Not In Love	Enrique Igelsias Kelis	SFMW852	12
Not Me Not I	Delta Goodrem	SFMW858	15
Not The Doctor	Alanis Morissette	SFMW840	11
Nothin' Bout Me	Genesis	SFMW828	07
Nothing Ever Hapeens	Del Amitri	SFMW825	08
Notorious	Loverboy	SFMW906	03
November Rain	Guns 'n' Roses	SFMW848	12
Novocaine For The Soul	Eels	SFMW893	03
Now And Forever	Richard Marx	SFMW829	08
Now Is The Time	Jimmy James And The Vagabonds	SFMW813	02
Now That I Know What I Want	Ronan Keating And Brian Kenne	SFMW872	08
Nowhere	Therapy	SFMW886	08

Title	Artist	Code	
Nowhere Man	Beatles	SFMW823	07
Numb	Linkin Park	SFMW863	10
Number Of The Beast	Iron Maiden	SFMW880	01
Octopus's Garden	Beatles	SFMW898	08
Oh Girl	Chi Lites	SFMW868	02
Oh Happy Days	Lauren Hill	SFMW843	09
Oh Julie	Shakin' Stevens	SFMW840	15
Oldest Swinger In Town	Fred Wedlock	SFMW894	11
Oliver's Army	Elvis Costello And The Attrac	SFMW920	06
On And On	Long Pigs	SFMW908	07
On Moonlight Bay	Doris Day	SFMW907	10
On My Radio	Selecter	SFMW882	05
On The Amazon	Don Mclean	SFMW919	15
On The Border	Al Stewart	SFMW875	02
On The Good Ship Lollipop	Shirley Temple	SFMW903	12
On The Wings Of A Nightingale	Everly Brothers	SFMW871	09
Once Bitten Twice Shy	Ian Hunter	SFMW926	09
Once In A Lifetime	Talking Heads	SFMW866	03
Once Upon A Long Ago	Paul Mccartney	SFMW870	01
One	Mary J Blige And U2	SFMW876	07
One	U2	SFMW921	08

Title	Artist	Code
One Day In Your Life	Michael Jackson	SFMW824 10
One Day Like This	Elbow	SFMW917 04
One In Ten	U B 40	SFMW812 11
One More Kiss Dear	Don Percival	SFMW909 07
One More Night	Phil Collins	SFMW827 09
One Piece At A Time	Johnny Cash	SFMW820 12
One Step Out Of Time	Michael Ball	SFMW826 14
One Vision	Queen	SFMW852 06
One Voice	Barry Manilow	SFMW828 08
One Way Or Another	Blondie	SFMW861 02
One Week	Barenaked Ladies	SFMW821 01
Only One I Know	Charlatans	SFMW864 04
Only To Be With You	Style Council	SFMW861 10
Only When You Leave	Spandau Ballet	SFMW814 08
Only You	Platters	SFMW923 12
Open Arms	Tina Moore	SFMW857 06
Open Up	Leftfield And Lydon	SFMW880 05
Open Your Heart	Madonna	SFMW893 10
Ordinary People	John Legend	SFMW869 01
Original Prankster	Offspring	SFMW807 14
Original Sin	Inxs	SFMW867 14
Orinoco Flow	Enya	SFMW840 10

Title	Artist	Code	Track
Orpheus	Ash	SFMW852	13
Our Day Will Come	Ruby And The Romantics	SFMW827	12
Out In The Fields	Gary Moore And Phil Lynott	SFMW882	03
Out Of Time	Chris Farlowe	SFMW821	05
Over My Shoulder	Mike And The Mechanics	SFMW802	06
Over You	Roxy Music	SFMW832	06
Overrated	Siobhan Donaghy	SFMW840	03
Oye Mi Canto	Gloria Estefan	SFMW830	12
Papa's Got A Brand New Bag	James Brown	SFMW931	08
Paper Plane	Status Quo	SFMW912	13
Paperback Writer	Beatles	SFMW818	01
Paranoid Android	Radiohead	SFMW809	09
Parisienne Walkways	Gary Moore	SFMW837	05
Part Time Love	Elton John	SFMW831	12
Party Town	Glen Feary	SFMW811	06
Pass The Dutchie	Musical Youth	SFMW842	15
Patience Of Angels	Eddi Reader	SFMW887	11
Patricia The Stripper	Chris De Burgh	SFMW840	07
Peek-a-boo	Siouxsie And The Banshees	SFMW888	11
Penny Arcade	Roy Orbison	SFMW867	15
People Are Strange	Doors	SFMW857	08

Title	Artist	Code	#
People Everyday	Arrested Development	SFMW865	08
Perfect Day	Hoku	SFMW875	03
Perfect Day	Susan Boyle	SFMW931	10
Perhaps Perhaps Perhaps	Doris Day	SFMW834	11
Pets	Porno For Pyros	SFMW902	04
Photograph	Ringo Starr	SFMW816	15
Piano In The Dark	Brenda Russell	SFMW828	09
Picture	Kid Rock-feat -sheryl Crow	SFMW930	05
Piece Of My Heart	Beverley Knight	SFMW876	06
Pieces Of Me	Ashlee Simpson	SFMW857	13
Pipes Of Peace	Paul Mccartney	SFMW838	14
Play Dead	Bjork And David Arnold	SFMW870	06
Playboy	Marvelettes	SFMW899	05
Playing With Fire	N-dubz Feat Mr Hudson	SFMW922	06
Please Don't Go	K C And The Sunshine Band	SFMW832	07
Please Read The Letter	Robert Plant And Alison Kraus	SFMW912	09
Please Stay	Crying Shames	SFMW817	02
Plug In Baby	Muse	SFMW860	01
Plush	Stone Temple Pilots	SFMW890	02
Poison Arrow	A B C	SFMW803	09
Pon De Replay	Rihanna	SFMW886	07
Pop Muzik	M	SFMW828	10

Title	Artist	Code
Power	Snap	SFMW861 05
Power Of Love	Jennifer Rush	SFMW862 05
Prayer	Anthony Callea	SFMW861 12
Pretend	Alvin Stardust	SFMW818 04
Prettiest Eyes	Beautiful South	SFMW858 03
Pretty Green Eyes	Ultrabeat	SFMW844 14
Pretty In Pink	Psychedelic Furs	SFMW847 11
Princes Of The Universe	Queen	SFMW896 01
Propane Nightmares	Pendulum	SFMW901 02
Protection	Massive Attack	SFMW893 12
Proud	Heather Small	SFMW865 07
Proud	Susan Boyle	SFMW921 02
Prowlin'	Adrian Zmed (Grease 2)	SFMW922 14
Puff The Magic Dragon	Peter Paul And Mary	SFMW840 08
Pump Up The Jam	Technotronic	SFMW805 01
Punk And The Godfather	Who	SFMW922 03
Push It	Salt 'n' Pepa	SFMW888 13
Pushbike Song	Mixtures	SFMW903 04
Put Your Money Where Your Mouth Is	Jet	SFMW885 06
Putting On The Ritz	Ella Fitzgerald	SFMW816 02
Pyt (Pretty Young Thing)	Michael Jackson	SFMW920 14

Title	Artist	Code
Que Sera Sera	Doris Day	SFMW801 09
Queen Of The New Year	Deacon Blue	SFMW857 03
Queer	Garbage	SFMW904 12
Questionnaire	Rutles	SFMW910 04
Quicksand	La Roux	SFMW915 04
Quiet Life	Japan	SFMW832 08
Race	Yello	SFMW888 05
Rain Or Shine	5 Star	SFMW878 10
Rainy Night In Georgia	Randy Crawford	SFMW899 08
Rappers Delight	Sugarhill Gang	SFMW873 01
Raspberry Beret	Prince	SFMW907 11
Rasputin	Boney M	SFMW875 12
Rat Trap	Boomtown Rats	SFMW854 03
Read 'em And Weep	Meat Loaf	SFMW811 08
Ready To Start	Arcade Fire	SFMW932 02
Real Man	Bonnie Raitt	SFMW904 13
Real Slim Shady	Eminem	SFMW804 01
Real Thing	Lisa Stansfield	SFMW802 08
Recipe For Love	Harry Jr Connick	SFMW890 14
Recover	Automatic	SFMW883 11
Red Light Spells Danger	Billy Ocean	SFMW811 11
Red Rain	Peter Gabriel	SFMW915 01

Title	Artist	Code
Red Strokes	Garth Brooks	SFMW856 07
Redemption Song	Bob Marley	SFMW923 10
Reelin' In The Years	Steely Dan	SFMW932 08
Reflections	Diana Ross And The Supremes	SFMW926 11
Regret	New Order	SFMW889 08
Regulate	Warren G And Nate Dogg	SFMW868 08
Rehab	Amy Winehouse	SFMW885 11
Release Me	Engelbert Humperdinck	SFMW849 06
Relight My Fire	Dan Hartman	SFMW830 13
Relight My Fire	Take That And Lulu	SFMW816 09
Remember (Walking In Thesand)	Shangri Las	SFMW869 12
Remember You're A Womble	Wombles	SFMW830 14
Resistance	Muse	SFMW931 14
Reviewing The Situation	Ron Moody (Oliver! Soundtrack)	SFMW916 11
Rhiannon	Fleetwood Mac	SFMW871 06
Rhythm Of The Rain	Cascades	SFMW803 14
Ribbon In The Sky	Stevie Wonder	SFMW916 12
Riddle	Nik Kershaw	SFMW839 15
Ride On Time	Black Box	SFMW817 09
Right Back Where We Started From	Maxine Nightingale	SFMW830 15
Right Or Wrong	Wanda Jackson	SFMW926 05

Title	Artist	Code
Ring Of Fire	Johnny Cash	SFMW815 06
Ring Ring	Dollar	SFMW802 13
Rio	Michael Nesmith	SFMW876 11
Rip Her To Shreds	Blondie	SFMW865 13
Rise	Gabrielle	SFMW845 10
River Runs Low	Bruce Hornsby And The Range	SFMW890 08
Riverboat Song	Ocean Color Scene	SFMW834 12
Rock And Roll Is King	Electric Light Orchestra	SFMW897 06
Rock Island Line	Lonnie Donegan	SFMW843 10
Rock Me Amadeus	Falco	SFMW835 10
Rock 'n' Roll High School	Ramones	SFMW864 13
Rocker	Ac Dc	SFMW890 03
Rocker	Thin Lizzy	SFMW906 01
Rocks	Primal Scream	SFMW854 04
Rockstar	Nickelback	SFMW895 13
Rocky Mountain High	John Denver	SFMW887 14
Rocky Racoon	Beatles	SFMW902 08
Romeo	Mr Big	SFMW867 02
Rooms On Fire	Stevie Nicks	SFMW897 12
Rooster	Alice In Chains	SFMW899 15
Rosalie	Thin Lizzy	SFMW896 07
Rosanna	Toto	SFMW855 12

Title	Artist	Code	
Roses Are Red My Love	Bobby Vinton	SFMW814	12
Roxette	Dr Feelgood	SFMW925	15
Ruby Tuesday	Melanie	SFMW802	11
Run	Snow Patrol	SFMW850	03
Run Baby Run	Sheryl Crow	SFMW809	15
Run For Home	Lindisfarne	SFMW832	09
Run Run Run	Jo Jo Gunne	SFMW910	01
Run To Him	Bobby Vee	SFMW813	05
Run To Me	Bee Gees	SFMW838	08
Run To You	Bryan Adams	SFMW882	02
Runaground	James	SFMW881	06
Running Up That Hill	Kate Bush	SFMW837	08
Running With The Night	Lionel Richie	SFMW869	11
Rush Hour	Jane Wiedlin	SFMW888	06
Rusty Cage	Soundgarden	SFMW903	01
S O S	Take That	SFMW932	13
Sad Lisa	Cat Stevens	SFMW847	04
Sailing	Rod Stewart	SFMW862	14
Saint Tropez	Ricky Martin	SFMW815	10
Same Ol' Love	Anita Baker	SFMW823	14
Same Old Song And Dance	Aerosmith	SFMW931	13

Song	Artist	Code	Track
San Quentin	Johnny Cash	SFMW847	06
Santa Baby	Madonna	SFMW918	16
Sarah	Thin Lizzy	SFMW903	03
Satellite	Hooters	SFMW879	07
Satellite Of Love	Lou Reed	SFMW858	14
Savin' Me	Nickelback	SFMW880	08
Say Hello Wave Goodbye	David Gray	SFMW835	02
Say Hello Wave Goodbye	Soft Cell	SFMW825	09
Say How I Feel	Rhian Benson	SFMW857	11
Say It Again	Natasha Bedingfield	SFMW898	13
Say Something	James	SFMW877	07
Scar Tissue	Red Hot Chili Peppers	SFMW848	01
School Days	Chuck Berry	SFMW931	05
Scooby Snacks	Fun Lovin' Criminals	SFMW868	09
Screamager	Therapy	SFMW887	03
Secrets That You Keep	Mud	SFMW822	02
See Emily Play	Pink Floyd	SFMW918	08
See The Day	D C Lee	SFMW847	10
See You Later Alligator	Bill Haley And His Comets	SFMW821	04
Seeker	Who	SFMW896	03
Self Control	Infernal	SFMW900	14
Self Preservation Society	Italian Job	SFMW882	04

Title	Artist	Code	
Senses Working Overtime	X T C	SFMW871	05
Sensual World	Kate Bush	SFMW896	11
Sergeant Peppers Lonely Heart Club	Beatles	SFMW866	01
Set Adrift On Memory Bliss	P M Dawn	SFMW859	15
Seven Seas	Echo And The Bunnymen	SFMW892	05
Seven Seas Of Rhye	Queen	SFMW811	07
Seven Tears	Goombay Dance Band	SFMW917	02
Sex And Drugs And Rock And Roll	Ian Dury And The Blockheads	SFMW808	06
Sex Machine	James Brown	SFMW805	11
Sexuality	Billy Bragg	SFMW877	13
Sexy Eyes	Dr Hook	SFMW808	04
Sgt Rock (Is Going To Help Me)	X T C	SFMW907	03
Shadow Of Love	Dammed	SFMW909	04
Shadow On The Wall	Mike Oldfield	SFMW914	07
Shake Shake Shake Shake	K C And The Sunshine Band	SFMW827	05
Shark In The Water	Vv Brown	SFMW930	12
Shattered Dreams	Johnny Hates Jazz	SFMW866	11
She Blinded Me With Science	Thomas Dolby	SFMW878	01
She Left Me On A Friday	Shed Seven	SFMW834	13
Sheer Heart Attack	Queen	SFMW899	09
She's A Mystery To Me	Roy Orbison	SFMW883	08

Title	Artist	Code	Track
She's Got Me Dancin'	Tommy Sparks	SFMW920	05
She's Got You	Patsy Cline	SFMW815	04
She's Leaving Home	Beatles	SFMW817	14
She's Like The Wind	Patrick Swayze	SFMW804	13
She's Madonna	Robbie Williams	SFMW886	12
She's Out Of My Life	Michael Jackson	SFMW840	06
She's Out Of My Life	Michael Jackson	SFMW841	16
Shine A Little Love	Electric Light Orchestra	SFMW911	02
Shining	Kristian Leontinou	SFMW856	01
Ships In The Night	Be Bop Deluxe	SFMW927	05
Shoot Me With Your Love	D Ream	SFMW817	11
Shooting Star	Dollar	SFMW914	10
Shout	Isley Brothers	SFMW827	02
Showing Out	Mel And Kim	SFMW910	13
Si Si Je Suis Un Rock Star	Bill Wyman	SFMW914	08
Sideboard Song	Chas And Dave	SFMW908	13
Sideways	Dierks Bentley	SFMW916	04
Sign Your Name	Terence Trent D'arby	SFMW852	09
Signed Sealed Delivered I'm Yours	Stevie Wonder	SFMW915	13
Silly Love Songs	Paul Mccartney	SFMW813	12
Silver Dream Machine	David Essex	SFMW825	10
Simon Smith And His Amazing Dancing	Alan Price	SFMW846	10

Title	Artist	Code	
Since Yeasterday	Strawberry Switchblade	SFMW909	12
Sinful	Peter Wylie	SFMW871	13
Sing For Absolution	Muse	SFMW853	01
Sister Christian	Night Ranger	SFMW873	09
Size Of A Cow	Wonder Stuff	SFMW885	02
Skin Deep	Stranglers	SFMW883	01
Skin Trade	Duran Duran	SFMW864	14
Skinny Genes	Eliza Doolittle	SFMW932	12
Sleepwalking	Maria Lawson	SFMW881	12
Slide Away	Oasis	SFMW802	04
Small Town Boy	Bronski Beat	SFMW829	05
Smells Like Teen Spirit	Nirvana	SFMW858	02
Snooker Loopy	Chas And Dave	SFMW833	13
So Beautiful	Simply Red	SFMW871	10
So Close	Dina Carroll	SFMW868	05
So Emotional	Whitney Houston	SFMW880	15
So Far Away	Dire Straits	SFMW884	01
Soldier Of Love	Donny Osmond	SFMW893	11
Solitary Man	Neil Diamond	SFMW862	03
Solsbury Hill	Peter Gabriel	SFMW909	06
Some Days Are Diamonds	John Denver	SFMW867	05

Title	Artist	Code
Some Girls	Rachel Stevens	SFMW857 07
Some Guys Have All The Luck	Rod Stewart	SFMW852 04
Some Like It Hot	Power Station	SFMW916 15
Someday	Mariah Carey	SFMW829 09
Something	Beatles	SFMW929 12
Something	Lasgo	SFMW839 06
Something For The Weekend	Divine Comedy	SFMW892 06
Something Inside So Strong	Labi Siffre	SFMW817 01
Something Old Something New	Fantastiks	SFMW819 14
Sometimes	Brand New Heavies	SFMW891 06
Sometimes	Eurasure	SFMW809 03
Somewhere Down The Crazy River	Robbie Robertson	SFMW888 15
Somewhere In The Night	Barry Manilow	SFMW836 01
Somewhere Only We Know	Keane	SFMW850 15
Song Bird	Eva Cassidy	SFMW811 14
Sonnet	Verve	SFMW809 10
Sooner Or Later	Larry Graham	SFMW899 10
Sould Provider	Michael Bolton	SFMW826 15
Sound	James	SFMW887 07
Sound Of The Crowd	Human League	SFMW869 07
Sowing The Seeds Of Love	Tears For Fears	SFMW811 05
Space Oddity	David Bowie	SFMW874 06

Title	Artist	Code	
Speak Now	Taylor Swift	SFMW930	15
Special Brew	Bad Manners	SFMW867	12
Special Years	Val Doonican	SFMW910	09
Speechless	Lady Gaga	SFMW925	14
Speedy Gonzales	Pat Boone	SFMW815	05
Spirit Of Radio	Rush	SFMW921	01
Spoonman	Soundgarden	SFMW884	08
Spread Your Wings	Queen	SFMW891	01
Stairway To Heaven	Rolf Harris	SFMW853	09
Stand	Rem	SFMW906	05
Stand By Me	Oasis	SFMW860	05
Stand By You	Pretenders	SFMW843	11
Stand By You	S Club 7	SFMW815	15
Stand Up For Love	Destiny's Child	SFMW873	07
Standing Alone	Tyketto	SFMW891	02
Star	Kiki Dee	SFMW828	11
Stardog Champion	Mother Love Bone	SFMW908	04
Starmaker	Kids From Fame	SFMW842	02
Starman	David Bowie	SFMW841	05
Stars	Dubstar	SFMW882	12
Starting Together	Su Pollard	SFMW907	07

Title	Artist	Code	
State Of Independence	Donna Summer	SFMW884	14
Stay	Dirty Dancing	SFMW816	13
Stay	Lisa Loeb And Nine Stories	SFMW839	08
Stay	Shakespear's Sister	SFMW845	05
Stay The Night	Ghosts	SFMW891	11
Stayin' Alive	Bee Gees	SFMW849	03
Staying Alive	N Trance	SFMW851	14
Steam	Peter Gabriel	SFMW931	03
Still	Commodores	SFMW922	09
Still The Same	Bob Seger	SFMW814	10
Stoned Love	Supremes	SFMW812	14
Stop	Erasure	SFMW846	01
Stop	Sam Brown	SFMW811	02
Stop Crying Your Heart Out	Leona Lewis	SFMW920	03
Storm Front	Billy Joel	SFMW828	12
Storm In A Teacup	Fortunes	SFMW822	14
Story Of My Life	Don Williams	SFMW819	07
Story Of My Life	Kristian Leontiou	SFMW853	13
Story Of The Blues	Wah	SFMW911	10
Strange Little Girl	Stranglers	SFMW879	09
Stranger In Moscow	Michael Jackson	SFMW922	11
Strawberry Fields Forever	Beatles	SFMW842	10

Title	Artist	Code
Street Life	Crusaders Feat Randy Crawford	SFMW922 08
Street Tuff	Rebel Mc	SFMW861 14
Streets Of Philadelphia	Bruce Springsteen	SFMW881 11
Strict Machine	Goldfrapp	SFMW887 05
Strut Your Funky Stuff	Frantique	SFMW829 10
Strutter	Kiss	SFMW927 13
Stuck Like Glue	Sugarland	SFMW928 11
Stumblin' In	Smokie And Suzie Quatro	SFMW808 03
Subterranean Homesick Blues	Bob Dylan	SFMW921 12
Suck My Kiss	Red Hot Chili Peppers	SFMW883 10
Suddenly	Angry Anderson	SFMW844 10
Suddenly I See	Kt Tunstall	SFMW870 02
Suedehead	Morrissey	SFMW856 10
Sugar Candy Kisses	Mac And Katie Kissoon	SFMW883 03
Sugar Mice	Marillion	SFMW904 14
Sugarman	Rodriguez	SFMW855 10
Suicide Is Painless	Theme From Mash	SFMW834 15
Sukiyaki	Kyu Sakamoto	SFMW824 06
Summer Girls	Lyte Funky Ones	SFMW875 15
Summer Love	Neil Diamond	SFMW904 04
Summer Love Sensation	Bay City Rollers	SFMW801 12

Title	Artist	Code
Summer Rain	Belinda Carlisle	SFMW846 06
Summertime	Sundays	SFMW903 14
Sun Always Shines On Tv	A Ha	SFMW817 07
Sunny	Bobby Hebb	SFMW823 10
Sunshine Day	Brady Bunch	SFMW914 09
Sunshine On Leith	Proclaimers	SFMW837 01
Sunshine Superman	Donovan	SFMW876 13
Superfreak	Rick James	SFMW880 12
Superhero	Jane's Addiction	SFMW908 05
Superman	Lazlo Bane	SFMW910 05
Superstar Tradesman	View	SFMW914 02
Superunknown	Soundgarden	SFMW890 01
Superwoman	Karyn White	SFMW884 13
Surrey With A Fringe On Top	Gordon Macrae	SFMW891 14
Susanna	Art Company	SFMW923 06
Sussudio	Phil Collins	SFMW870 04
Sweet Child O' Mine	Taken By Trees	SFMW919 12
Sweet Dreams	Patsy Cline	SFMW860 15
Sweet Emotion	Aerosmith	SFMW854 08
Sweet Gene Vincent	Ian Dury And The Blockheads	SFMW926 12
Sweet Home Alabama	Lynyrd Skynyrd	SFMW850 06
Sweet Leaf	Black Sabbath	SFMW931 02

Title	Artist	Code
Sweet Lorraine	Uriah Heap	SFMW909 03
Sweet Talkin' Guy	Chiffons	SFMW913 08
Sweet Talkin' Woman	Electric Light Orchestra	SFMW822 15
Sweetest Taboo	Sade	SFMW816 14
Swing Low Sweet Chariot	U B 40	SFMW847 13
Swinging On A Star	Bing Crosby	SFMW814 15
Sympathy For The Devil	Rolling Stones	SFMW858 13
Symphony Of Life	Tina Arena	SFMW868 14
System Addict	Five Star	SFMW834 14
Take Me As I Am	Faith Hill	SFMW836 11
Take Me Back 'ome	Slade	SFMW813 09
Take Me Home Country Roads	John Denver	SFMW802 10
Take Me Out	Franz Ferdinand	SFMW849 13
Take Your Mama	Scissor Sisters	SFMW852 02
Talk Of The Town	Pretenders	SFMW914 13
Talk Talk	Talk Talk	SFMW843 12
Talk To Me	Stevie Nicks	SFMW836 04
Teardrop	Massive Attack	SFMW891 10
Telegram Sam	T Rex	SFMW811 10
Telephone Line	Electric Light Orchestra	SFMW901 14
Tell Her About It	Billy Joel	SFMW847 07

Title	Artist	Code	Track
Tell Her No	Zombies	SFMW845	11
Tell Her This	Del Amitri	SFMW899	13
Tell Me I'm Crazy	Shelby Lynn	SFMW871	14
Temptaion Waits	Garbage	SFMW889	05
Ten Out Of Ten	Paolo Nutini	SFMW927	11
Tequila	Alt And The Lost Civilisation	SFMW865	01
Tequila Sunrise	Eagles	SFMW823	02
Tesla Girls	Omd	SFMW870	15
Thank God It's Christmas	Queen	SFMW858	01
Thank You Baby	Shania Twain	SFMW849	15
Thank You For Being A Friend (Golde	Andrew Gold	SFMW903	07
Thank You For The Years	Shirley Bassey	SFMW900	08
That Old Devil Called Love	Alison Moyet	SFMW820	07
That Same Old Feeling	Pikketywitch	SFMW822	06
That Sounds Good To Me	Josh Dubovie	SFMW927	12
That Thing You Do	Lauren Hill	SFMW847	03
That's All	Genesis	SFMW827	08
That's All Right	Elvis Presley	SFMW854	07
That's What Friends Are For	Deniece Williams	SFMW925	02
That's What Friends Are For	Dionne Warwick And Friends	SFMW829	11
Theme From Shaft	Isaac Hayes	SFMW872	02
There Goes The Fear	Doves	SFMW930	07

Title	Artist	Code	#
There Is A Light That Never Goes Ou	Smiths	SFMW839	12
There Must Be An Angel	Eurythmics	SFMW817	06
There There	Radiohead	SFMW838	07
There You Go	Pink	SFMW882	16
There's A Ghost In My House	R Dean Taylor	SFMW878	12
There's No Business Like Show Busin	Annie Get Your Gun	SFMW894	13
There's No Other Way	Blur	SFMW817	10
There's Nothing Like This	Omar	SFMW856	09
These Dreams	Heart	SFMW924	13
These Foolish Things	Bryan Ferry	SFMW926	08
They Don't Really Care About Us	Michael Jackson	SFMW803	10
Thing Called Love	Darkness	SFMW845	15
Things Can Only Get Better	Howard Jones	SFMW908	02
Things That Make You Go Hmmmm	C And C Music Factory	SFMW893	08
Things We Do For Love	10cc	SFMW832	11
Thinking Of You	Colourfield	SFMW900	11
Thinking Of You	Paul Weller	SFMW858	06
This Corrosion	Sisters Of Mercy	SFMW889	01
This Is How We Do It	Montell Jordan	SFMW843	13
This Is It	Melba Moore	SFMW822	08
This Is My Life	Shirley Bassey	SFMW919	14

Title	Artist	Code	
This Is The Life	Amy Macdonald	SFMW898	03
This Old Heart Of Mine	Isley Brothers	SFMW801	03
This Ole House	Shakin' Stevens	SFMW833	15
This Woman's Work	Kate Bush	SFMW899	12
Thousand Stars	Kathy Young And The Innocents	SFMW876	10
Three Bells	Browns	SFMW820	02
Three Little Birds	Bob Marley	SFMW811	09
Three Times A Lady	Commodores	SFMW847	09
Thrill Is Gone	B B King	SFMW880	13
Thriller	Michael Jackson	SFMW840	05
Through The Barricades	Spandau Ballet	SFMW807	07
Thunder In My Heart	Leo Sayer	SFMW874	04
Thunder Road	Bruce Springsteen	SFMW853	02
Thunderstruck	Ac Dc	SFMW805	03
Tied To The 90's	Travis	SFMW842	12
Till There Was You (From The Music	Shirley Jones	SFMW913	07
Time For Action	Secret Affair	SFMW878	05
Time Has Come	Adam Faith	SFMW865	14
Time Is Running Out	Muse	SFMW856	04
Time Of Your Life	Green Day	SFMW867	11
Time Will Pass You By	Tobi Legend	SFMW911	05
Times Like These	Foo Fighters	SFMW845	14

Title	Artist	Code
Tiny Dancer	Elton John	SFMW920 04
Tired Of Being Alone	Al Green	SFMW808 10
To All The Girls I've Loved Before	Julio Iglesias And Willie Nel	SFMW819 08
To Be Someone	Jam	SFMW898 06
To Know Him Is To Love Him	Teddy Bears	SFMW827 13
To Love Again	Alesha Dixon	SFMW919 09
To Sir With Love	Lulu	SFMW886 11
Today	Smashing Pumpkins	SFMW917 07
Toes	Zac Brown Band	SFMW919 02
Together In Electric Dreams	Giorio Moroder And Phil Oader	SFMW841 13
Tom's Diner	Suzanne Vega	SFMW895 02
Too Blind To See It	Kym Sims	SFMW837 06
Too Many Broken Hearts	Jason Donovan	SFMW930 10
Total Control	Motels	SFMW824 15
Touchy	A Ha	SFMW888 07
Towers Of London	X T C	SFMW869 05
Toxicity	System Of A Down	SFMW930 04
Toy Boy	Sinitta	SFMW905 06
Toy Soldier	Martika	SFMW846 08
Train In Vain (Stand By Me)	Clash	SFMW889 06
Trains And Boats And Planes	Anita Harris	SFMW819 06

Title	Artist	Code	
Transmission	Joy Division	SFMW913	10
Trash	Suede	SFMW932	04
Travelin' Soldier	Dixie Chicks	SFMW908	12
Treat Her Like A Lady	Temptations	SFMW923	08
Tribute	Tenacious D	SFMW849	10
Tribute (Right On)	Pasadenas	SFMW908	10
Trick Of Tail	Genesis	SFMW828	13
Trigger Hippie	Morcheeba	SFMW915	05
Trouble	Lindsey Buckingham	SFMW867	03
True Faith	New Order	SFMW846	03
Try	Nelly Furtado	SFMW855	03
Try Again	Aaliyah	SFMW804	15
Tug Of War	Paul Mccartney	SFMW896	06
Tunnel Of Love	Fun Boy Three	SFMW914	05
Turn Back The Clock	Johnny Hates Jazz	SFMW814	05
Turn It On Again	Genisis	SFMW871	03
Turn It Up	Pixie Lott	SFMW928	06
Turn The Beat Around	Gloria Estefan	SFMW882	10
Turn The Page	Rush	SFMW902	01
Turn To Stone	Electric Light Orchestra	SFMW879	11
Twent Four Sycamore	Gene Pitney	SFMW816	06
Twenty Flight Rock	Eddie Cochran	SFMW811	13

Title	Artist	Code	
Twistin The Night Away	Sam Cooke	SFMW855	14
Two Hearts	Phil Collins	SFMW809	11
Two Is Better Than One	Boys Like Girls Feat Taylor S	SFMW919	13
Two Little Boys	Rolf Harris	SFMW851	13
Two Storey House	George Jones And Tammy Wynett	SFMW916	03
U Can't Touch This	Mc Hammer	SFMW831	14
Ullo John Got A New Motor	Alexei Sayle	SFMW846	12
Una Paloma Blanca	Jonathan King	SFMW872	11
Under Your Thumb	Godley And Creme	SFMW868	04
Unfinshed Sympathy	Massive Attack	SFMW874	14
Uninvited	Alanis Morissette	SFMW893	01
Universal	Blur	SFMW905	12
Until The End Of The World	U2	SFMW864	12
Up Up And Away	5th Dimension	SFMW895	08
Upside Down	Diana Ross	SFMW889	10
Upside Down	Jack Johnson	SFMW877	04
Us And Them	Pink Floyd	SFMW910	12
Valentine	T'pau	SFMW911	03
Valerie	Steve Winwood	SFMW861	13
Vasoline	Stone Temple Pilots	SFMW884	07
Vaya Con Dios	Paul Les And Mary Ford	SFMW895	14

Title	Artist	Code	Track
Venus	Frankie Avalon	SFMW801	06
Vice	Razorlight	SFMW862	10
Video Killed The Radio Star	Buggles	SFMW835	11
Video Killed The Radio Star	Presidents Of The Usa	SFMW913 ✓	11
Visions In Blue	Ultravox	SFMW913	14
Visions Of China	Japan	SFMW927	07
Vogue	Madonna	SFMW845	07
Voice	Ultravox	SFMW862	09
Volare	Dean Martin	SFMW801	15
Voodoo Child	Rogue Traders	SFMW878	08
Wait 'till You See My Smile	Alicia Keys	SFMW932	09
Waiting For An Alibi	Thin Lizzy	SFMW890	04
Waiting For The End	Linkin Park	SFMW930	02
Waiting In Vain	Bob Marley	SFMW833	02
Walk Away	Cast	SFMW848	04
Walk Away Renee	Four Tops	SFMW801	07
Walk In The Park	Nick Straker Band	SFMW891	04
Walk Like A Panther	All Seeing Eye Feat Tony Chri	SFMW864	02
Walk Of Life	Dire Straits	SFMW851	03
Walking On The Sun	Smash Mouth	SFMW841	15
Walking Wounded	Everything But The Girl	SFMW911	06
Wall Street Shuffle	10cc	SFMW814	01

Title	Artist	Code	
Wanted	Dooleys	SFMW822	07
War	Edwin Star	SFMW805	07
War Pigs	Black Sabbath	SFMW928	01
Warm Wet Circles	Marillion	SFMW903	08
Wasted Little Djs	View	SFMW908	09
Watching You	Rogue Traders	SFMW881	07
Watercolour	Pendulum	SFMW925	01
Waterfront	Simple Minds	SFMW829	13
Way I Feel	Roachford	SFMW833	14
Way It Is	Bruce Hornsby And The Range	SFMW854	05
Way You Make Me Feel	Michael Jackson	SFMW889	07
We Are Detective	Thompson Twins	SFMW886	03
We Are Glass	Gary Numan	SFMW911	14
We Built This City	Starship	SFMW855	08
We Care A Lot	Faith No More	SFMW878	03
We Don't Cry Out Loud	Elkie Brooks	SFMW918	06
We Don't Talk Anymore	Cliff Richard	SFMW925	11
We Have All The Time In The World	Louis Armstrong	SFMW867	01
We Weren't Born To Follow	Bon Jovi	SFMW919	01
We Wish You A Merry Christmas	Traditional (Brass Band And C	SFMW918	13
Weak	Skunk Anansie	SFMW865	05

Title	Artist	Code
Welcome To Paradise	Green Day	SFMW917 01
Welcome To The Cheap Seats	Wonderstuff	SFMW841 03
We'll Meet Again	Vera Lynn	SFMW882 18
We're All In This Together	High School Musical	SFMW926 15
We're Gonna Change The World	Matt Monro	SFMW880 10
We're In This Love Together	Al Jarreau	SFMW823 11
We've Got A Good Thing Going	Sugar Minnott	SFMW850 09
What A Differece A Day Makes	Dinah Washington	SFMW815 01
What A Waste	Ian Dury And The Blockheads	SFMW857 15
What Becomes Of The Broken Hearted	Jimmy Ruffin	SFMW916 06
What Can I Say	Boz Craggs	SFMW801 10
What Have I Done To Deserve This	Pet Shop Boys And Dusty Sprin	SFMW836 15
What I Like About You	Romantics	SFMW872 01
What Is This Feeling?	Kristin Chenoweth-and-idina M	SFMW932 15
What I've Been Looking For	High School Musical	SFMW928 15
What Made You Say That	Shania Twain	SFMW836 09
What The World Needs Now Is Love	Jackie Deshannon	SFMW819 03
Whatever I Do (Wherever I Go)	Hazell Dean	SFMW915 03
Wheels Of Steel	Saxon	SFMW842 05
When I Fall In Love	Nat King Cole	SFMW887 13
When I'm Cleaning Windows	George Formby	SFMW862 15
When It's Love	Van Halen	SFMW888 04

Title	Artist	Code
When Love Breaks Down	Prefab Sprout	SFMW909 05
When October Goes	Barry Manilow	SFMW828 14
When Smokey Sings	A B C	SFMW801 11
When The Lights Go Out	Five	SFMW831 13
When The Ship Comes In	Bob Dylan	SFMW863 15
When We Was Fab	George Harrison	SFMW897 03
When Will I Be Famous	Bros	SFMW844 11
When Will I Be Loved	Linda Ronstadt	SFMW925 13
When Will I See You Again	Three Degrees	SFMW811 01
When Will The Good Apples Fall	Seekers	SFMW910 07
When You Say Nothing At All	Alison Krauss And Union Stati	SFMW917 10
When You Wish Upon A Star	Standard	SFMW803 06
When You're Mad	Ne Yo	SFMW906 07
When You're Young And In Love	Marvelettes	SFMW898 05
Whenever I Say Your Name	Sting And Mary J Blige	SFMW848 02
Where Are You Baby	Betty Boo	SFMW913 06
Where Are You Christmas	Faith Hill	SFMW844 12
Where I Find My Heaven	Gigolo Aunts	SFMW900 12
Where Is My Mind	Piranhas	SFMW857 05
Where My Heart Will Take Me	Russell Watson	SFMW842 13
Where The Wild Roses Grow	Nick Cave And Kylie Minogue	SFMW862 13

Title	Artist	Code
Wherever I May Roam	Metallica	SFMW927 01
Whistle For The Choir	Fratellis	SFMW884 02
White Horses	Jackie Lee	SFMW881 08
Who Do You Think You Are	Spice Girls	SFMW867 13
Who Gonna Rock You Now	Nolans	SFMW898 09
Whoa	Lil Kim	SFMW905 10
Whole Lotta Love	Led Zeppelin	SFMW804 10
Whoopsie Daisy	Terri Walker	SFMW863 07
Who's Holding Donna Now	Debarge	SFMW808 02
Who's Leaving Who	Hazell Dean	SFMW885 09
Who's That Girl	Eurythmics	SFMW831 15
Who's That Girl	Madonna	SFMW807 02
Why	Bronski Beat	SFMW880 04
Why Does It Hurt So Bad	Whitney Houston	SFMW824 03
Why Don't You Give Me Your Love	Zutons	SFMW876 01
Wide Open Space	Mansun	SFMW873 05
Wide Open Spaces	Dixie Chicks	SFMW890 15
Wild Horses	Sundays	SFMW889 09
Wild Side Of Life	Status Quo	SFMW801 08
Wild West Hero	Electric Light Orchestra	SFMW881 02
Winter Winds	Mumford-and-sons	SFMW929 04
Winters Tale	David Essex	SFMW833 01

Title	Artist	Code
Winterwood	Don Mclean	SFMW918 05
Wish You Were Here	Pink Floyd	SFMW866 07
Wishfull Thinking	China Crisis	SFMW801 13
Wishing Well	Terence Trent D'arby	SFMW807 12
With One Look	Michael Ball	SFMW842 08
With Or Without You	U2	SFMW837 09
Without You	Harry Nilsson	SFMW818 12
Wives And Lovers	Jack Jones	SFMW819 04
Woman From Tokyo	Deep Purple	SFMW894 03
Woman In Love	Three Degrees	SFMW913 05
Wonderboy	Tenacious D	SFMW843 14
Wonderful Christmastime	Paul Mccartney	SFMW930 17
Wonderful World Beautiful People	Jimmy Cliff	SFMW857 12
Wonderous Stories	Yes	SFMW910 14
Wonderwall	Mike Flowers Pops	SFMW883 14
Wood Beez	Scritti Politti	SFMW915 02
Wooly Bully	Sam The Man And The Pharaohs	SFMW816 08
Word Called Love	Johnny Cash	SFMW835 03
Word Girl	Scritti Politti	SFMW887 10
Word Up	Cameo	SFMW920 13
Words	F R David	SFMW814 04

World In My Eyes	Depeche Mode	SFMW851 09
World Is Outside	Ghosts	SFMW890 13
Wot Do You Call It	Wiley	SFMW851 15
Wow	Kate Bush	SFMW900 05
X Offender	Blondie	SFMW897 14
Year Of The Cat	Al Stewart	SFMW930 06
Years From Now	Dr Hook	SFMW822 11
Yeh Yeh Yeh	Mel C	SFMW844 13
Yes Sir I Can Boogie	Baccara	SFMW909 14
Ying Tong Song	Goons	SFMW835 06
You And Me Song	Wannadies	SFMW865 09
You Are	Lionel Richie	SFMW836 08
You Belong To The City	Glenn Frey	SFMW812 15
You Bring The Sun Out	Crawford Randy	SFMW901 06
You Came	Kim Wilde	SFMW866 15
You Can Call Me Al	Paul Simon	SFMW853 04
You Can Leave Your Hat On	Tom Jones	SFMW828 15
You Could Be Happy	Snow Patrol	SFMW912 10
You Do Something To Me	Paul Weller	SFMW809 08
You Got It	Roy Orbison	SFMW882 14
You Got The Love	Source Feat Candi Staton	SFMW874 01
You Got The Style	Athlete	SFMW912 11

Title	Artist	Code
You Keep Me Hangin' On	Supremes	SFMW895 11
You Make Me Feel Like A Natural Wom	Aretha Franklin	SFMW860 13
You Make Me Sick	Pink	SFMW885 14
You Need Me	Mariah Carey	SFMW829 15
You Only Live Twice	Nancy Sinatra	SFMW878 11
You Oughta Know	Alanis Morissette	SFMW807 15
You Really Got Me	Van Halen	SFMW803 13
You Think You're A Man	Divine	SFMW914 03
You Wear It Well	Rod Stewart	SFMW861 07
You'll Accompany Me	Bob Seger And The Silver Bull	SFMW924 09
You'll Never Get To Heaven	Dionne Warwick	SFMW819 09
You'll Never Know	Hi Gloss	SFMW832 13
Young And Beautiful	Elvis Presley	SFMW848 11
Your Love Is King	Sade	SFMW823 15
Your Song	Euan Mcgregor	SFMW835 01
You're A Lady	Peter Skellern	SFMW903 09
You're History	Shakespear's Sister	SFMW907 05
You're My Everything	Temptations	SFMW924 08
You're My Heart You're My Soul	Modern Talking	SFMW922 07
You're The Best	Joe Esposito	SFMW923 02
You're The Best Thing	Style Council	SFMW832 12

Title	Artist	Code
You've Got To Hide Your Love Away	Beatles	SFMW820 03
Zing Went The Strings Of My Heart	Trammps	SFMW820 06
Zoom	Fat Larrys Band	SFMW806 06
Zoot Suit	High Numbers	SFMW897 10

IN ORDER OF ARTIST

When requesting a song write down

Your Name

The Song Name (eg. 2 minutes to midnight)

The Artist Name (eg. Iron Maiden)

The code (eg SFMW889)

the track number (eg. 02)

please make sure you have
all that information before handing to the DJ

ARTIST	SONG	MF CODE	TRACK
10cc	Things We Do For Love	SFMW832	11
10cc	Wall Street Shuffle	SFMW814	01
30 Seconds To Mars	Kings And Queens	SFMW920	07
5 Star	Rain Or Shine	SFMW878	10
5th Dimension	Aquarius Let The Sunshine In	SFMW880	06
5th Dimension	Up Up And Away	SFMW895	08
A B C	Poison Arrow	SFMW803	09
A B C	When Smokey Sings	SFMW801	11
A Ha	Hunting High And Low	SFMW820	15
A Ha	Sun Always Shines On Tv	SFMW817	07
A Ha	Touchy	SFMW888	07
Aaliyah	Try Again	SFMW804	15
Abba	Hasta Manana	SFMW929	05
Ac Dc	Back In Black	SFMW883	13
Ac Dc	Big Gun	SFMW932	01
Ac Dc	For Those About To Rock	SFMW817	04
Ac Dc	Heatseeker	SFMW882	13
Ac Dc	Hells Bells	SFMW863	08
Ac Dc	It's A Long Way To The Top	SFMW879	03
Ac Dc	Let There Be Rock	SFMW880	07
Ac Dc	Rocker	SFMW890	03

Artist	Title	Code
Ac Dc	Thunderstruck	SFMW805 03
Adam Faith	Time Has Come	SFMW865 14
Adamski	Killer	SFMW844 08
Adrian Zmed (Grease 2)	Prowlin'	SFMW922 14
Adventures Of Stevie V	Dirty Cash	SFMW905 07
Aerosmith	Dude (Looks Like A Lady)	SFMW862 07
Aerosmith	Love In An Elevator	SFMW805 12
Aerosmith	Same Old Song And Dance	SFMW931 13
Aerosmith	Sweet Emotion	SFMW854 08
A-ha	Cry Wolf	SFMW918 02
Air	All I Need	SFMW877 15
Al Green	Tired Of Being Alone	SFMW808 10
Al Jarreau	Moonlighting	SFMW834 09
Al Jarreau	We're In This Love Together	SFMW823 11
Al Stewart	On The Border	SFMW875 02
Al Stewart	Year Of The Cat	SFMW930 06
Alan Jackson	Chattahoochee	SFMW821 02
Alan Jackson And Jimmy Buffet	It's Five O'clock Somewhere	SFMW854 11
Alan Price	Simon Smith And His Amazing Dancing	SFMW846 10
Alanis Morissette	All I Really Want	SFMW839 02
Alanis Morissette	Everything	SFMW852 15
Alanis Morissette	I See Right Through You	SFMW834 08

Artist	Title	Code
Alanis Morissette	Ironic	SFMW809 13
Alanis Morissette	Not The Doctor	SFMW840 11
Alanis Morissette	Uninvited	SFMW893 01
Alanis Morissette	You Oughta Know	SFMW807 15
Alarm	68 Guns	SFMW889 03
Albert Hammond	Free Electric Band	SFMW866 13
Albert King	Born Under A Bad Sign	SFMW881 14
Alesha Dixon	To Love Again	SFMW919 09
Alex Parks	Looking For Water	SFMW872 12
Alexander O'neal	Criticize	SFMW842 14
Alexander O'neal	If You Were Here Tonight	SFMW845 12
Alexei Sayle	Ullo John Got A New Motor	SFMW846 12
Alice Cooper	Feed My Frankenstein	SFMW893 09
Alice Cooper	Hey Stoopid	SFMW897 13
Alice Deejay	I Want You Back In My Life	SFMW838 12
Alice In Chains	No Excuses	SFMW877 01
Alice In Chains	Rooster	SFMW899 15
Alicia Keys	No One	SFMW896 13
Alicia Keys	Wait 'till You See My Smile	SFMW932 09
Alison Krauss	It Doesn't Matter	SFMW890 07
Alison Krauss And Union Stati	When You Say Nothing At All	SFMW917 10

Artist	Title	Code
Alison Moyet	All Cried Out	SFMW820 09
Alison Moyet	Love Insurrection	SFMW814 09
Alison Moyet	Love Letters	SFMW820 10
Alison Moyet	That Old Devil Called Love	SFMW820 07
All 4 One	I Swear	SFMW916 13
All About Eve	Martha's Harbour	SFMW888 09
All Saints	I Know Where It's At	SFMW885 10
All Seeing Eye Feat Tony Chri	Walk Like A Panther	SFMW864 02
All Time Low	Dear Maria Count Me In	SFMW931 04
Alt And The Lost Civilisation	Tequila	SFMW865 01
Alvin Stardust	Pretend	SFMW818 04
Ami Stewart	Knock On Wood	SFMW827 07
Amy Macdonald	Mr Rock And Roll	SFMW899 07
Amy Macdonald	This Is The Life	SFMW898 03
Amy Winehouse	Rehab	SFMW885 11
Andrew Gold	Never Let Her Slip Away	SFMW808 05
Andrew Gold	Thank You For Being A Friend (Golde	SFMW903 07
Andy Williams	Can't Take My Eyes Off You	SFMW815 08
Angry Anderson	Suddenly	SFMW844 10
Anita Baker	Same Ol' Love	SFMW823 14
Anita Harris	Trains And Boats And Planes	SFMW819 06
Annie Get Your Gun	There's No Business Like Show Busin	SFMW894 13

Artist	Title	Code	Track
Anthony Callea	Prayer	SFMW861	12
Arcade Fire	Ready To Start	SFMW932	02
Arctic Monkeys	I Bet You Look Good On The Danceflo	SFMW871	01
Arctic Monkeys	Mardy Bum	SFMW921	07
Aretha Franklin	Baby I Love You	SFMW911	08
Aretha Franklin	Don't Play That Song	SFMW841	14
Aretha Franklin	You Make Me Feel Like A Natural Wom	SFMW860	13
Arrested Development	People Everyday	SFMW865	08
Art Company	Susanna	SFMW923	06
Arthur Askey	Bee Song (Busy Bee)	SFMW904	09
Ash	Orpheus	SFMW852	13
Ashlee Simpson	Autobiography	SFMW873	03
Ashlee Simpson	Pieces Of Me	SFMW857	13
Assembly	Never Never	SFMW925	08
Asteroids Galaxy Tour	Around The Bend	SFMW920	02
Aswad	Don't Turn Around	SFMW809	06
Athlete	El Salvador	SFMW908	11
Athlete	You Got The Style	SFMW912	11
Audioslave	Cochise	SFMW865	15
Automatic	Recover	SFMW883	11
Avril Lavigne	Keep Holding On	SFMW886	15

Artist	Song	Code
Avril Lavigne	Nobody's Fool	SFMW855 06
B B King	How Blue Can You Get	SFMW894 08
B B King	Thrill Is Gone	SFMW880 13
Baby D	Let Me Be Your Fantasy	SFMW817 08
Babyface-feat -stevie Wonder	How Come How Long	SFMW932 06
Baccara	Yes Sir I Can Boogie	SFMW909 14
Bachman-turner Overdrive	Hey You	SFMW901 03
Backstreet Boys	Get Another Boyfriend	SFMW843 02
Bad Company	Can't Get Enough (Of Your Love)	SFMW924 02
Bad Manners	Special Brew	SFMW867 12
Bananarama	Cruel Summer	SFMW923 05
Band Perry	If I Die Young	SFMW931 12
Bangles	Going Down To Liverpool	SFMW902 11
Bangles	Hero Takes A Fall	SFMW896 12
Bangles	If She Knew What She Wants	SFMW887 08
Bangles	In Your Room	SFMW893 04
Barbara Dickson	Caravan Song	SFMW821 03
Barenaked Ladies	One Week	SFMW821 01
Barry Manilow	It's A Miracle	SFMW836 02
Barry Manilow	Mandy	SFMW920 11
Barry Manilow	One Voice	SFMW828 08
Barry Manilow	Somewhere In The Night	SFMW836 01

Artist	Title	Code
Barry Manilow	When October Goes	SFMW828 14
Barry Ryan	Eloise	SFMW900 04
Barry White	Just The Way You Are	SFMW812 07
Barry White	Let The Music Play	SFMW809 01
Baseballs	I Don't Feel Like Dancin'	SFMW929 15
Basement Jaxx	Good Luck	SFMW857 10
Bauhaus	Kick In The Eye	SFMW840 14
Bay City Rollers	Give A Little Love	SFMW822 05
Bay City Rollers	Summer Love Sensation	SFMW801 12
Be Bop Deluxe	Ships In The Night	SFMW927 05
Beach Boys	Barbara Ann	SFMW829 03
Beach Boys	California Girls	SFMW832 03
Beach Boys	Fun Fun Fun	SFMW859 13
Beach Boys	God Only Knows	SFMW855 09
Beach Boys	Good Vibrations	SFMW830 04
Beach Boys	I Can Hear Music	SFMW824 12
Beastie Boys	Fight For Your Right To Party	SFMW852 07
Beat	Mirror In The Bathroom	SFMW867 04
Beatles	Across The Universe	SFMW906 11
Beatles	And Your Bird Can Sing	SFMW896 10
Beatles	Being For The Benefit Of Mr Kite	SFMW901 04

Beatles	Blackbird	SFMW925 03
Beatles	Day In The Life	SFMW859 05
Beatles	Day Tripper	SFMW850 04
Beatles	Don't Let Me Down	SFMW824 08
Beatles	Eleanor Rigby	SFMW842 09
Beatles	Here Comes The Sun	SFMW872 05
Beatles	I'm Only Sleeping	SFMW899 11
Beatles	In My Life	SFMW839 05
Beatles	Lady Madonna	SFMW801 01
Beatles	Let It Be	SFMW823 06
Beatles	Long And Winding Road	SFMW823 09
Beatles	Love Me Do	SFMW823 08
Beatles	Lovely Rita	SFMW875 08
Beatles	Nowhere Man	SFMW823 07
Beatles	Octopus's Garden	SFMW898 08
Beatles	Paperback Writer	SFMW818 01
Beatles	Rocky Racoon	SFMW902 08
Beatles	Sergeant Peppers Lonely Heart Club	SFMW866 01
Beatles	She's Leaving Home	SFMW817 14
Beatles	Something	SFMW929 12
Beatles	Strawberry Fields Forever	SFMW842 10
Beatles	You've Got To Hide Your Love Away	SFMW820 03

Artist	Title	Code
Beatmasters And Betty Boo	Hey Dj I Can't Dance To That Music	SFMW893 07
Beats International	Dub Be Good To Me	SFMW852 10
Beautiful South	Prettiest Eyes	SFMW858 03
Bee Gees	Jive Talkin'	SFMW929 06
Bee Gees	Run To Me	SFMW838 08
Bee Gees	Stayin' Alive	SFMW849 03
Beetlejuice	Jump In Line (Shake Shake)	SFMW837 12
Belinda Carlisle	Leave A Light On	SFMW864 03
Belinda Carlisle	Live Your Life Be Free	SFMW903 06
Belinda Carlisle	Summer Rain	SFMW846 06
Ben Folds Five	Battle Of Who Could Care Less	SFMW866 12
Ben Folds Five	Brick	SFMW839 10
Betty Boo	Doin' The Do	SFMW839 04
Betty Boo	Where Are You Baby	SFMW913 06
Beverley Knight	Come As You Are	SFMW877 10
Beverley Knight	Piece Of My Heart	SFMW876 06
Biffy Clyro	Bubbles	SFMW928 12
Biffy Clyro	Captain	SFMW930 03
Biffy Clyro	God And Satan	SFMW929 02
Biffy Clyro	Many Of Horror	SFMW931 15
Biffy Clyro	Mountains	SFMW919 03

Artist	Title	Code
Big Bopper	Chantilly Lace	SFMW816 07
Big Country	King Of Emotion	SFMW888 03
Big Pink	Dominos	SFMW920 01
Bill Haley And His Comets	See You Later Alligator	SFMW821 04
Bill Withers	Ain't No Sunshine	SFMW804 11
Bill Wyman	Si Si Je Suis Un Rock Star	SFMW914 08
Billie Holiday	Gloomy Sunday	SFMW914 06
Billie Jo Spears	57 Chevrolet	SFMW819 15
Billy Bragg	New England	SFMW861 08
Billy Bragg	Sexuality	SFMW877 13
Billy Idol	Hot In The City	SFMW814 11
Billy Joel	All About Soul	SFMW823 13
Billy Joel	Leningrad	SFMW855 11
Billy Joel	Minor Variation	SFMW826 12
Billy Joel	Storm Front	SFMW828 12
Billy Joel	Tell Her About It	SFMW847 07
Billy Joel And Ray Charles	Baby Grand	SFMW826 02
Billy Ocean	Red Light Spells Danger	SFMW811 11
Bing Crosby	Do You Hear What I Hear	SFMW894 09
Bing Crosby	Swinging On A Star	SFMW814 15
Bjork	Army Of Me	SFMW932 07
Bjork And David Arnold	Play Dead	SFMW870 06

Artist	Song	Code	
Black Box	Ride On Time	SFMW817	09
Black Eyed Peas	My Humps	SFMW874	12
Black Grape	In The Name Of The Father	SFMW898	12
Black Lace	Gang Bang	SFMW834	05
Black Sabbath	Iron Man	SFMW926	01
Black Sabbath	Sweet Leaf	SFMW931	02
Black Sabbath	War Pigs	SFMW928	01
Bloc Party	Banquet	SFMW925	06
Blondie	Hanging On The Telephone	SFMW853	05
Blondie	One Way Or Another	SFMW861	02
Blondie	Rip Her To Shreds	SFMW865	13
Blondie	X Offender	SFMW897	14
Blue Oyster Cult	Don't Fear The Reaper	SFMW869	13
Blur	Beetlebum	SFMW873	15
Blur	There's No Other Way	SFMW817	10
Blur	Universal	SFMW905	12
Bob Dylan	Blowin' In The Wind	SFMW931	11
Bob Dylan	Forever Young	SFMW838	06
Bob Dylan	It's All Over Now Baby Blue	SFMW869	03
Bob Dylan	Like A Rolling Stone	SFMW924	11
Bob Dylan	Subterranean Homesick Blues	SFMW921	12

Artist	Title	Code
Bob Dylan	When The Ship Comes In	SFMW863 15
Bob Marley	Buffalo Soldier	SFMW805 08
Bob Marley	Could You Be Loved	SFMW889 14
Bob Marley	Get Up Stand Up	SFMW828 05
Bob Marley	Is This Love	SFMW834 10
Bob Marley	Jammin'	SFMW805 09
Bob Marley	No Woman No Cry	SFMW856 03
Bob Marley	Redemption Song	SFMW923 10
Bob Marley	Three Little Birds	SFMW811 09
Bob Marley	Waiting In Vain	SFMW833 02
Bob Seger	Still The Same	SFMW814 10
Bob Seger And The Silver Bull	Mainstreet	SFMW923 09
Bob Seger And The Silver Bull	You'll Accompany Me	SFMW924 09
Bobby Darin	18 Yellow Roses	SFMW876 12
Bobby Darin	Beyond The Sea	SFMW860 11
Bobby Darin	Don't Rain On My Parade	SFMW882 15
Bobby Hebb	Sunny	SFMW823 10
Bobby Vee	Run To Him	CFMW813 05
Bobby Vinton	Roses Are Red My Love	SFMW814 12
Bodyrockers	I Like The Way	SFMW867 08
Bomb The Bass	Don't Make Me Wait	SFMW888 10

Artist	Song	Code
Bon Jovi	All About Loving You	SFMW843 01
Bon Jovi	Livin' On A Prayer	SFMW838 04
Bon Jovi	We Weren't Born To Follow	SFMW919 01
Boney M	Belfast	SFMW804 08
Boney M	Brown Girl In The Ring	SFMW809 14
Boney M	Daddy Cool	SFMW808 01
Boney M	Ma Baker	SFMW829 07
Boney M	Rasputin	SFMW875 12
Bonnie Raitt	Love Letter	SFMW919 11
Bonnie Raitt	Real Man	SFMW904 13
Bonnie Tyler	It's A Heartache	SFMW804 12
Boomtown Rats	Rat Trap	SFMW854 03
Boston	More Than A Feeling	SFMW920 08
Boys Like Girls Feat Taylor S	Two Is Better Than One	SFMW919 13
Boyz 2 Men	4 Seasons Of Loneliness	SFMW932 10
Boyz 2 Men	End Of The Road	SFMW853 08
Boz Craggs	What Can I Say	SFMW801 10
Brady Bunch	Sunshine Day	SFMW914 09
Brand New Heavies	Sometimes	SFMW891 06
Brandy	I Tried	SFMW861 11
Bratt	Chalk Dust	SFMW833 04
Bravery	Honest Mistake	SFMW864 05

Artist	Title	Code
Breathe	Hands To Heaven	SFMW888 08
Breeders	Cannonball	SFMW868 01
Brenda Lee	I Want To Be Wanted	SFMW878 15
Brenda Lee	If You Love Me	SFMW816 03
Brenda Russell	Piano In The Dark	SFMW828 09
Brian Mcknight	Back At One	SFMW928 08
Britney Spears	Beat Goes On	SFMW815 09
Britney Spears	Break The Ice	SFMW900 13
Britney Spears	Email My Heart	SFMW815 12
Britney Spears	I Will Be There	SFMW815 11
Bronski Beat	Small Town Boy	SFMW829 05
Bronski Beat	Why	SFMW880 04
Brook Benton	House Is Not A Home	SFMW819 01
Brooks And Dunn	Boot Scootin' Boogie	SFMW926 14
Bros	I Owe You Nothing	SFMW807 03
Bros	When Will I Be Famous	SFMW844 11
Brother Beyond	Harder I Try	SFMW911 11
Brotherhood Of Man	Angelo	SFMW834 01
Browns	Three Bells	SFMW820 02
Bruce Hornsby And The Range	River Runs Low	SFMW890 08
Bruce Hornsby And The Range	Way It Is	SFMW854 05

Artist	Title	Code
Bruce Springsteen	Cover Me	SFMW836 05
Bruce Springsteen	Human Touch	SFMW836 06
Bruce Springsteen	Streets Of Philadelphia	SFMW881 11
Bruce Springsteen	Thunder Road	SFMW853 02
Bryan Adams	18 Till I Die	SFMW803 11
Bryan Adams	Flying	SFMW859 02
Bryan Adams	Heaven	SFMW883 09
Bryan Adams	Run To You	SFMW882 02
Bryan Ferry	Hard Rain's Gonna Fall	SFMW902 02
Bryan Ferry	These Foolish Things	SFMW926 08
Bucks Fizz	Land Of Make Believe	SFMW818 02
Bucks Fizz	My Camera Never Lies	SFMW840 04
Buggles	Video Killed The Radio Star	SFMW835 11
Bugsy Malone	Bugsy Malone	SFMW864 06
Burl Ives	Big Rock Candy Mountain	SFMW928 07
Burt Bacharack And Elvis Cost	Give Me Strength	SFMW819 12
Busted	3 00 Am	SFMW853 06
C And C Music Factory	Things That Make You Go Hmmmm	SFMW893 08
Cab Calloway	Minnie The Moocher	SFMW812 01
Cameo	Word Up	SFMW920 13
Captain And Tennille	Do That To Me One More Time	SFMW924 10
Captain Sensible	Happy Talk	SFMW817 05

Artist	Title	Code
Cardigans	My Favourite Game	SFMW855 15
Carly Simon	Let The River Run	SFMW926 07
Carly Simon	Nobody Does It Better	SFMW850 05
Carmel	More More More	SFMW828 03
Carol Bayer Sager	Moving Out Today	SFMW878 14
Carrie Underwood	All American Girl	SFMW927 09
Carrie Underwood	Jesus Take The Wheel	SFMW890 12
Carrie Underwood	Last Name	SFMW926 10
Cars	My Best Friends Girl	SFMW808 09
Cascada	Everytime We Touch	SFMW924 07
Cascades	Rhythm Of The Rain	SFMW803 14
Cast	Walk Away	SFMW848 04
Cat Stevens	Matthew And Son	SFMW915 07
Cat Stevens	Moonshadow	SFMW905 04
Cat Stevens	Sad Lisa	SFMW847 04
Celine Dion	All By Myself	SFMW852 03
Celine Dion	Miles To Go	SFMW841 11
Change	Lover's Holiday	SFMW871 08
Chapman And Knight	Love Is A Battlefield	SFMW863 05
Charlatans	Only One I Know	SFMW864 04
Charles Penrose	Laughing Policeman	SFMW905 05

Artist	Title	Code
Charlie Daniels	Devil Went Down To Georgia	SFMW801 04
Charlie Rich	Behind Closed Doors	SFMW815 03
Chas And Dave	Gertcha	SFMW874 10
Chas And Dave	Sideboard Song	SFMW908 13
Chas And Dave	Snooker Loopy	SFMW833 13
Cheers	Cheers	SFMW803 05
Cheryl Lynn	Got To Be Real	SFMW827 06
Chi Lites	Oh Girl	SFMW868 02
Chiffons	Sweet Talkin' Guy	SFMW913 08
China Crisis	Wishfull Thinking	SFMW801 13
Chordettes	Lollipop	SFMW915 09
Chris De Burgh	Don't Pay The Ferryman	SFMW875 09
Chris De Burgh	Patricia The Stripper	SFMW840 07
Chris Farlowe	Out Of Time	SFMW821 05
Chris Isaak	Blue Hotel	SFMW900 09
Chris Rea	Julia	SFMW918 15
Chuck Berry	Johnny B Goode	SFMW862 02
Chuck Berry	School Days	SFMW931 05
Citykiss	Detroit Rock	SFMW923 01
Clash	Guns Of Brixton	SFMW909 01
Clash	I Fought The Law	SFMW849 11

Artist	Title	Code
Clash	London Calling	SFMW806 03
Clash	Train In Vain (Stand By Me)	SFMW889 06
Cliff Richard	Day I Met Marie	SFMW825 11
Cliff Richard	We Don't Talk Anymore	SFMW925 11
Coast To Coast	Do The Hucklebuck	SFMW826 04
Cockerel Chorus	Nice One Cyril	SFMW818 08
Colleen Hewett	Dreaming My Dreams With You	SFMW883 05
Colourfield	Thinking Of You	SFMW900 11
Commodores	Lady	SFMW833 12
Commodores	Still	SFMW922 09
Commodores	Three Times A Lady	SFMW847 09
Connie Francis	Everybody's Somebody's Fool	SFMW879 13
Connie Francis	Lipstick On Your Collar	SFMW866 10
Coral	Dreaming Of You	SFMW853 12
Corinne Bailey-rae	I'd Do It All Again	SFMW922 12
Counting Crows	Mr Jones	SFMW833 10
Craig David	Don't Love You No More (I'm Sorry)	SFMW877 09
Crash Test Dummies	Afternoons And Coffee Spoons	SFMW877 08
Crawford Randy	You Bring The Sun Out	SFMW901 06
Cream	I Feel Free	SFMW843 04
Creedence Clearwater Revival	Bad Moon Rising	SFMW871 04

Artist	Title	Code
Crosby Stills Nash And Young	Love The One You're With	SFMW924 03
Crosby Stills Nash And Young	Marrakesh Express	SFMW855 07
Cross Section	Hi Heel Sneekers	SFMW878 04
Crowded House	Four Seasons In One Day	SFMW881 04
Crusaders Feat Randy Crawford	Street Life	SFMW922 08
Crying Shames	Please Stay	SFMW817 02
Cure	Boys Don't Cry	SFMW835 07
Cure	Close To Me	SFMW856 02
Cure	In Between Days	SFMW915 08
Cure	Love Cats	SFMW808 08
Cure	Lullaby	SFMW912 03
Curtis Mayfield	Move On Up	SFMW862 12
Curtis Stigers	I Wonder Why	SFMW802 07
D C Lee	See The Day	SFMW847 10
D Ream	Shoot Me With Your Love	SFMW817 11
Damage	Forever	SFMW850 13
Damien Rice	Blower's Daughter	SFMW860 06
Damien Rice	Cannonball	SFMW918 04
Dammed	Shadow Of Love	SFMW909 04
Damned	New Rose	SFMW847 02
Dan Hartman	Relight My Fire	SFMW830 13

Artist	Title	Code
Dana	All Kinds Of Everything	SFMW898 10
Dana	It's Gonna Be A Cold Cold Christmas	SFMW918 18
Dandy Warhols	Bohemian Like You	SFMW839 14
Daniel Boone	Beautiful Sunday	SFMW821 06
Daniel O'donnell	Footsteps	SFMW859 08
Daniel O'donnell	Forty Shades Of Green	SFMW851 12
Daniel Powter	Free Loop	SFMW872 14
Danny Wilson	Mary's Prayer	SFMW924 01
Darius Rucker	Come Back Song	SFMW930 11
Darius Rucker	History In The Making	SFMW926 13
Darkness	Girlfriend	SFMW876 05
Darkness	Growing On Me	SFMW847 15
Darkness	Thing Called Love	SFMW845 15
Darren Hayes	Darkness	SFMW860 10
Darts	Boy From New York City	SFMW828 01
Darts	Come Back My Love	SFMW818 15
Darts	Daddy Cool	SFMW820 04
Darts	It's Raining	SFMW907 06
Daryl Hall And John Oates	Maneater	SFMW809 02
Dave Clark Five	Because	SFMW827 11
David Bowie	Fashion	SFMW820 14

Artist	Title	Code
David Bowie	Golden Years	SFMW859 10
David Bowie	It Ain't Easy	SFMW838 03
David Bowie	Man Who Sold The World	SFMW897 01
David Bowie	Modern Love	SFMW924 06
David Bowie	Space Oddity	SFMW874 06
David Bowie	Starman	SFMW841 05
David Cassidy	Last Kiss	SFMW838 09
David Dundas	Jeans On	SFMW822 12
David Essex	Silver Dream Machine	SFMW825 10
David Essex	Winters Tale	SFMW833 01
David Gray	Say Hello Wave Goodbye	SFMW835 02
David Jordan	Move On	SFMW901 11
Deacon Blue	Fergus Sings The Blues	SFMW821 07
Deacon Blue	I'll Never Fall In Love Again	SFMW864 08
Deacon Blue	Queen Of The New Year	SFMW857 03
Dean Martin	Ain't That A Kick In The Head	SFMW921 14
Dean Martin	Everybody Loves Somebody	SFMW887 15
Dean Martin	It's Beginning To Look A Lot Like C	SFMW918 17
Dean Martin	Volare	SFMW801 15
Dean Martin And H O'connell	How Do You Like Your Eggs In The Mo	SFMW870 03
Dean Parrish	I'm On My Way	SFMW921 06

Artist	Title	Code
Debarge	Who's Holding Donna Now	SFMW808 02
Dee Lite	Groove Is In The Heart	SFMW806 01
Deep Dish	Flashdance	SFMW859 07
Deep Purple	Fireball	SFMW904 15
Deep Purple	Never Before	SFMW895 10
Deep Purple	Woman From Tokyo	SFMW894 03
Deepest Blue	Give It Away	SFMW851 08
Def Leppard	Animal	SFMW896 14
Def Leppard	Let's Get Rocked	SFMW885 07
Del Amitri	Driving With The Brakes On	SFMW878 13
Del Amitri	Here And Now	SFMW895 04
Del Amitri	Kiss This Thing Goodbye	SFMW837 07
Del Amitri	Nothing Ever Hapeens	SFMW825 08
Del Amitri	Tell Her This	SFMW899 13
Del Shannon	Kelly	SFMW864 15
Delta Goodrem	Not Me Not I	SFMW858 15
Deniece Williams	That's What Friends Are For	SFMW925 02
Denise Williams	Let's Hear It For The Boy	SFMW831 10
Department S	Is Vic There	SFMW905 14
Depeche Mode	Enjoy The Silence	SFMW862 06
Depeche Mode	World In My Eyes	SFMW851 09

Artist	Song	Code
Destiny's Child	Stand Up For Love	SFMW873 07
Diana Ross	Chain Reaction	SFMW825 15
Diana Ross	Upside Down	SFMW889 10
Diana Ross And The Supremes	Reflections	SFMW926 11
Dierks Bentley	Sideways	SFMW916 04
Dina Carroll	Ain't No Man	SFMW830 01
Dina Carroll	So Close	SFMW868 05
Dinah Washington	Mad About The Boy	SFMW910 10
Dinah Washington	What A Differece A Day Makes	SFMW815 01
Dion Warwick	I'll Never Fall In Love Again	SFMW874 15
Dionne Warwick	Alfie	SFMW819 10
Dionne Warwick	You'll Never Get To Heaven	SFMW819 09
Dionne Warwick And Friends	That's What Friends Are For	SFMW829 11
Dire Straits	Brothers In Arms	SFMW817 03
Dire Straits	Money For Nothing	SFMW865 06
Dire Straits	So Far Away	SFMW884 01
Dire Straits	Walk Of Life	SFMW851 03
Dirty Dancing	Loverboy	SFMW837 11
Dirty Dancing	Stay	SFMW816 13
Dirty Pretty Things	Bang Bang You're Dead	SFMW923 04
Divine	You Think You're A Man	SFMW914 03

Artist	Title	Code
Divine Comedy	Becoming More Like Alfie	SFMW893 05
Divine Comedy	Something For The Weekend	SFMW892 06
Dixie Chicks	Travelin' Soldier	SFMW908 12
Dixie Chicks	Wide Open Spaces	SFMW890 15
Dixie Cups	Chapel Of Love	SFMW902 12
Dj Bobo	Chihuahua	SFMW841 09
Dj Casper	Cha Cha Slide	SFMW851 05
Dj Sammy	Heaven (Slow Version)	SFMW837 10
Dobie Gray	Drift Away	SFMW932 17
Dollar	Give Me Back My Heart	SFMW909 09
Dollar	Loves Got A Hold Of Me	SFMW813 08
Dollar	Mirror Mirror	SFMW829 14
Dollar	Ring Ring	SFMW802 13
Dollar	Shooting Star	SFMW914 10
Dolly Parton	Here You Come Again	SFMW822 04
Dolly Parton	Joshua	SFMW885 12
Dolly Parton	Love Is Like A Butterfly	SFMW904 08
Dolly Parton	My Blue Ridge Mountin Boy	SFMW886 06
Don Henley	New York Minute	SFMW892 13
Don Mclean	On The Amazon	SFMW919 15
Don Mclean	Winterwood	SFMW918 05

Artist	Title	Code
Don Percival	One More Kiss Dear	SFMW909 07
Don Williams	Story Of My Life	SFMW819 07
Donna Summer	State Of Independence	SFMW884 14
Donny Osmond	Soldier Of Love	SFMW893 11
Donovan	Mellow Yellow	SFMW904 07
Donovan	Sunshine Superman	SFMW876 13
Dooleys	Wanted	SFMW822 07
Doors	Break On Through To The Other Side	SFMW926 03
Doors	People Are Strange	SFMW857 08
Doris Day	Black Hills Of Dakota	SFMW916 08
Doris Day	Deadwood Stage	SFMW889 11
Doris Day	On Moonlight Bay	SFMW907 10
Doris Day	Perhaps Perhaps Perhaps	SFMW834 11
Doris Day	Que Sera Sera	SFMW801 09
Doris Troy	Just One Look	SFMW824 05
Doves	Black And White Town	SFMW865 03
Doves	There Goes The Fear	SFMW930 07
Dr Feelgood	Roxette	SFMW925 15
Dr Hook	Cover Of Rolling Stone	SFMW819 13
Dr Hook	Everybody's Makin' It Big But Me	SFMW853 14
Dr Hook	I Don't Want To Be Alone Tonight	SFMW822 10

Artist	Title	Code
Dr Hook	In Over My Head	SFMW858 11
Dr Hook	More Like The Movies	SFMW822 09
Dr Hook	Sexy Eyes	SFMW808 04
Dr Hook	Years From Now	SFMW822 11
Drake	Find Your Love	SFMW930 09
Dream Warriors	My Definition Of A Boombastic Jazz	SFMW893 13
Drifters	Down On The Beach	SFMW819 11
Drums	Let's Go Surfing	SFMW928 04
Dubstar	Stars	SFMW882 12
Duran Duran	Hungry Like The Wolf	SFMW816 10
Duran Duran	Skin Trade	SFMW864 14
Dusty Springfield	Look Of Love	SFMW819 02
Dusty Springfield	Losing You	SFMW889 12
Eagles	Desperado	SFMW883 15
Eagles	Long Run	SFMW926 02
Eagles	Love Will Keep Us Alive	SFMW876 02
Eagles	Tequila Sunrise	SFMW823 02
Earth Wind And Fire	After The Love Has Gone	SFMW814 07
East 17	House Of Love	SFMW849 08
Echo And The Bunnyman	Killing Moon	SFMW851 10
Echo And The Bunnymen	Bring On The Dancing Horses	SFMW919 05

Artist	Title	Code
Echo And The Bunnymen	Killing Moon (Original Version)	SFMW854 10
Echo And The Bunnymen	Lips Like Sugar	SFMW921 04
Echo And The Bunnymen	Seven Seas	SFMW892 05
Eddi Reader	Patience Of Angels	SFMW887 11
Eddie And The Hot Rods	Do Anything You Wanna Do	SFMW806 04
Eddie Cochran	Twenty Flight Rock	SFMW811 13
Eddie Holman	Hey There Lonely Girl	SFMW816 04
Eddy Grant	Do You Feel My Love	SFMW808 07
Eddy Grant	Electric Avenue	SFMW805 04
Eddy Grant	I Don't Wanna Dance	SFMW805 05
Edith Piaf	La Vie En Rose	SFMW901 08
Editors	All Sparks	SFMW925 05
Editors	Bullets	SFMW874 13
Editors	Munich	SFMW919 08
Edwin Star	War	SFMW805 07
Edwin Starr	H A P P Y Radio	SFMW916 05
Eels	Mr E's Beautiful Blues	SFMW923 07
Eels	Novocaine For The Soul	SFMW893 03
Elastica	Connection	SFMW845 09
Elbow	One Day Like This	SFMW917 04
Electric Light Orchestra	Birmingham Blues	SFMW898 11

Artist	Title	Code
Electric Light Orchestra	Confusion	SFMW899 01
Electric Light Orchestra	Diary Of Horrace Wimp	SFMW835 08
Electric Light Orchestra	Do Ya	SFMW912 01
Electric Light Orchestra	Hold On Tight	SFMW885 01
Electric Light Orchestra	Is This The Way Life's Meant To Be	SFMW906 14
Electric Light Orchestra	Ma Ma Ma Belle	SFMW896 15
Electric Light Orchestra	Rock And Roll Is King	SFMW897 06
Electric Light Orchestra	Shine A Little Love	SFMW911 02
Electric Light Orchestra	Sweet Talkin' Woman	SFMW822 15
Electric Light Orchestra	Telephone Line	SFMW901 14
Electric Light Orchestra	Turn To Stone	SFMW879 11
Electric Light Orchestra	Wild West Hero	SFMW881 02
Electronic	Get The Message	SFMW884 12
Electronic	Getting Away With It	SFMW893 14
Elgins	Heaven Must Have Sent You	SFMW817 12
Eliza Doolittle	Skinny Genes	SFMW932 12
Elkie Brooks	We Don't Cry Out Loud	SFMW918 06
Ella Fitzgerald	Putting On The Ritz	SFMW816 02
Ellie Goulding	Guns And Horses	SFMW927 08
Elton John	Captain Fantastic And The Brown Dir	SFMW907 04
Elton John	Circle Of Life	SFMW806 07

Artist	Title	Code
Elton John	Crocodile Rock	SFMW821 08
Elton John	I'm Still Standing	SFMW823 12
Elton John	Lucy In The Sky With Diamonds	SFMW827 15
Elton John	Part Time Love	SFMW831 12
Elton John	Tiny Dancer	SFMW920 04
Elvin Bishop	Fooled Around And Fell In Love	SFMW898 07
Elvis Costello	I Can't Stand Up (For Falling Down)	SFMW904 06
Elvis Costello And The Attrac	Oliver's Army	SFMW920 06
Elvis Presley	Big Hunk O' Love	SFMW803 03
Elvis Presley	Don't Leave Me Now	SFMW803 01
Elvis Presley	I Just Can't Help Believing	SFMW857 02
Elvis Presley	I Wanna Be Free	SFMW803 02
Elvis Presley	If I Can Dream	SFMW837 13
Elvis Presley	Mess Of Blues	SFMW803 04
Elvis Presley	That's All Right	SFMW854 07
Elvis Presley	Young And Beautiful	SFMW848 11
Embrace	Come Back To What You Know	SFMW867 07
Embrace	Gravity	SFMW859 01
Eminem	Real Slim Shady	SFMW804 01
En Vogue	Don't Let Go	SFMW804 03
En Vogue	Free Your Mind	SFMW834 04

Artist	Title	Code
En Vogue	My Lovin' (You're Never Gonna Get I	SFMW833 11
Engelbert Humperdinck	Release Me	SFMW849 06
Engelbert Humperdink	Man Without Love	SFMW856 13
Enrique Igelsias Kelis	Not In Love	SFMW852 12
Enrique Iglesias-feat -nichol	Heartbeat	SFMW929 03
Enya	May It Be (Fellowship Of The Rings)	SFMW844 09
Enya	Orinoco Flow	SFMW840 10
Erasure	Little Respect	SFMW807 09
Erasure	Stop	SFMW846 01
Eric Clapton	Behind The Mask	SFMW871 11
Eric Clapton	Blues Power	SFMW838 02
Eric Clapton	Motherless Children	SFMW895 01
Euan Mcgregor	Your Song	SFMW835 01
Eurasure	Sometimes	SFMW809 03
Eurythmics	Here Comes The Rain Again	SFMW830 06
Eurythmics	It's Alright Baby's Coming Back	SFMW896 09
Eurythmics	There Must Be An Angel	SFMW817 06
Eurythmics	Who's That Girl	SFMW831 15
Eva Cassidy	Fields Of Gold	SFMW855 02
Eva Cassidy	Song Bird	SFMW811 14
Evanescence	Bring Me To Life	SFMW840 02

Artist	Title	Code
Evanescence	Going Under	SFMW897 04
Evanescence	Lithium	SFMW886 14
Evanescence	My Immortal	SFMW849 07
Everly Brothers	On The Wings Of A Nightingale	SFMW871 09
Everything But The Girl	I Don't Want To Talk About It	SFMW809 07
Everything But The Girl	Walking Wounded	SFMW911 06
Everything Everything	My Kz Ur Bf	SFMW929 08
Example	Kickstarts	SFMW927 14
Extreme	Get The Phunk Out	SFMW879 01
F R David	Words	SFMW814 04
Fairground Attraction	Find My Love	SFMW844 15
Faith Hill	Breathe	SFMW836 12
Faith Hill	Take Me As I Am	SFMW836 11
Faith Hill	Where Are You Christmas	SFMW844 12
Faith No More	Midlife Crisis	SFMW894 15
Faith No More	We Care A Lot	SFMW878 03
Falco	Rock Me Amadeus	SFMW835 10
Fantasia	I Believe	SFMW856 11
Fantastiks	Something Old Something New	SFMW819 14
Farley Jackmaster Funk	Love Can't Turn Around	SFMW903 05
Fat Larrys Band	Zoom	SFMW806 06

Artist	Title	Code
Fatboy Slim And Macy Gray	Demons	SFMW906 13
Feist	1234	SFMW894 01
Fergie	Big Girls Don't Cry	SFMW898 14
Fergie	London Bridge	SFMW885 05
Fiction Factory	Feels Like Heaven	SFMW825 02
Fine Young Cannibals	Good Thing	SFMW864 09
Fine Young Cannibals	Johnny Come Home	SFMW871 02
First Class	Beach Baby	SFMW802 12
Five	When The Lights Go Out	SFMW831 13
Five Satins	In The Still Of The Night	SFMW821 09
Five Star	System Addict	SFMW834 14
Fleetwood Mac	Big Love	SFMW836 03
Fleetwood Mac	Rhiannon	SFMW871 06
Flight Of The Conchords	Hiphopapotamus Vs Rhymenocerous	SFMW908 16
Flight Of The Conchords	I'm Not Crying	SFMW915 15
Flight Of The Conchords	Ladies Of The World	SFMW909 15
Flight Of The Conchords	Most Beautiful Girl	SFMW910 15
Flock Of Seagulls	I Ran	SFMW861 15
Florence And The Machine	Cosmic Love	SFMW927 03
Florence And The Machine	Dog Days Are Over	SFMW925 09
Florence And The Machine	Kiss With A Fist	SFMW907 12

Artist	Title	Code
Foo Fighters	All My Life	SFMW851 11
Foo Fighters	Everlong	SFMW893 02
Foo Fighters	Learn To Fly	SFMW833 09
Foo Fighters	Monkey Wrench	SFMW882 01
Foo Fighters	My Hero	SFMW892 03
Foo Fighters	Times Like These	SFMW845 14
Fortunes	Freedom Come Freedom Go	SFMW822 13
Fortunes	Storm In A Teacup	SFMW822 14
Four Aces	Mr Sandman	SFMW880 09
Four Tops	Loco In Acapulco	SFMW863 14
Four Tops	Walk Away Renee	SFMW801 07
Frank Sinatra	Embraceable You	SFMW915 12
Frank Sinatra	Love's Been Good To Me	SFMW882 17
Frankie Avalon	Venus	SFMW801 06
Frankie Laine	Cool Water	SFMW825 01
Frankie Laine	Jezebel	SFMW863 03
Frankie Miller	Darling	SFMW806 05
Frankie Valli	Night	SFMW816 05
Frantique	Strut Your Funky Stuff	SFMW829 10
Franz Ferdinand	Can't Stop Feeling	SFMW860 14
Franz Ferdinand	Take Me Out	SFMW849 13

Artist	Title	Code
Fratellis	Flathead	SFMW887 06
Fratellis	Whistle For The Choir	SFMW884 02
Fred Wedlock	Oldest Swinger In Town	SFMW894 11
Freddie Mercury	Living On My Own	SFMW804 04
Freddie Mercury And Montserra	Barcelona	SFMW860 07
Freeze	I O U	SFMW833 07
Freiheit	Keeping The Dream Alive	SFMW930 16
Fun Boy Three	Tunnel Of Love	SFMW914 05
Fun Lovin' Criminals	Scooby Snacks	SFMW868 09
Fun Loving Criminals	Loco	SFMW896 05
Gabrielle	Rise	SFMW845 10
Gap Band	Big Fun	SFMW844 01
Garbage	Queer	SFMW904 12
Garbage	Temptaion Waits	SFMW889 05
Garth Brooks	Callin' Baton Rouge	SFMW924 14
Garth Brooks	Red Strokes	SFMW856 07
Gary Miller	Aqua Marina	SFMW901 05
Gary Moore	Parisienne Walkways	SFMW837 05
Gary Moore And Phil Lynott	Out In The Fields	SFMW882 03
Gary Numan	We Are Glass	SFMW911 14
Gary Wright	Dream Weaver	SFMW892 08

Artist	Title	Code	#
Gene Pitney	If I Didn't Have A Dime	SFMW824	13
Gene Pitney	Nobody Needs Your Love	SFMW861	09
Gene Pitney	Twent Four Sycamore	SFMW816	06
Genesis	Follow You Follow Me	SFMW844	06
Genesis	I Can't Dance	SFMW804	06
Genesis	In Too Deep	SFMW827	10
Genesis	Jesus He Knows You	SFMW839	11
Genesis	Keep It Dark	SFMW897	02
Genesis	Mama	SFMW828	06
Genesis	No Son Of Mine	SFMW865	11
Genesis	Nothin' Bout Me	SFMW828	07
Genesis	That's All	SFMW827	08
Genesis	Trick Of Tail	SFMW828	13
Genisis	Turn It On Again	SFMW871	03
George Baker Collection	Little Green Bag	SFMW872	15
George Benson	In Your Eyes	SFMW820	01
George Formby	When I'm Cleaning Windows	SFMW862	15
George Harrison	Give Me Love	SFMW825	04
George Harrison	Isn't It A Pity	SFMW904	05
George Harrison	When We Was Fab	SFMW897	03
George Jones And Tammy Wynett	Two Storey House	SFMW916	03

Artist	Title	Code
George Mccr'	It's Been So Long	SFMW802 15
George Michael	Heal The Pain	SFMW826 08
Gerard Mcmann	Cry Little Sister (From The Lost Bo	SFMW913 15
Gerry And The Pacemakers	Ferry 'cross The Mersey	SFMW857 14
Gerry Rafferty	Baker Street	SFMW860 02
Gerry Rafferty	Night Owl	SFMW869 02
Ghosts	Stay The Night	SFMW891 11
Ghosts	World Is Outside	SFMW890 13
Gigolo Aunts	Where I Find My Heaven	SFMW900 12
Giorio Moroder And Phil Oader	Together In Electric Dreams	SFMW841 13
Gladys Knight	Licence To Kill	SFMW845 01
Glass Tiger	My Town	SFMW907 01
Cloe Cast	Alone	SFMW924 15
Glee Cast	Deck The Rooftop	SFMW930 01
Glee Cast	Gold Digger	SFMW923 15
Glee Cast	Halo Walking On Sunshine	SFMW922 15
Glen Campbell	Gentle On My Mind	SFMW886 02
Glen Feary	Party Town	SFMW811 06
Glenn Frey	Heat Is On	SFMW803 15
Glenn Frey	You Belong To The City	SFMW812 15
Gloria Estefan	Don't Wanna Lose You	SFMW809 12

Artist	Song	Code	Track
Gloria Estefan	Get On Your Feet	SFMW876	08
Gloria Estefan	Oye Mi Canto	SFMW830	12
Gloria Estefan	Turn The Beat Around	SFMW882	10
Gloria Gaynor	Honeybee	SFMW910	08
Gloria Gaynor	I Am What I Am	SFMW804	07
Gloria Gaynor	Never Can Say Goodbye	SFMW801	02
Go West	Call Me	SFMW868	07
Godley And Creme	Under Your Thumb	SFMW868	04
Goldfrapp	Strict Machine	SFMW887	05
Gonzalez	I Haven't Stopped Dancing Yet	SFMW868	11
Goo Goo Dolls	Iris	SFMW846	02
Good Charlotte	Keep Your Hands Off My Girl	SFMW886	13
Goodies	Funky Gibbon	SFMW825	03
Goodies	Goodies Theme	SFMW826	07
Goombay Dance Band	Seven Tears	SFMW917	02
Goons	Ying Tong Song	SFMW835	06
Gordon Macrae	Surrey With A Fringe On Top	SFMW891	14
Gorillaz	El Manana	SFMW879	12
Gorillaz	Kids With Guns	SFMW877	02
Grandmaster Flash	Message	SFMW806	13
Grease	Grease Megamix	SFMW881	15

Artist	Title	Code
Green Day	American Idiot	SFMW857 01
Green Day	Basket Case	SFMW849 04
Green Day	Jesus Of Suburbia	SFMW873 06
Green Day	Longview	SFMW918 01
Green Day	Time Of Your Life	SFMW867 11
Green Day	Welcome To Paradise	SFMW917 01
Guns 'n' Roses	November Rain	SFMW848 12
Gwen Mccrae	All This Love That I'm Giving	SFMW905 09
Hall And Oates	Kiss On My List	SFMW918 11
Halo James	Could Have Told You So	SFMW919 07
Hank Williams	Hey Good Lookin	SFMW821 10
Hannah Montana	He Could Be The One	SFMW928 14
Hard-fi	Hard To Beat	SFMW923 03
Harry Chapin	Cat's In The Cradle	SFMW827 14
Harry Connick Jnr	It Had To Be You	SFMW826 10
Harry Enfield	Loads A Money	SFMW830 07
Harry Jr Connick	Recipe For Love	SFMW890 14
Harry Nilsson	Everybody's Talkin'	SFMW818 06
Harry Nilsson	Without You	SFMW818 12
Hazel O'connor	Eighth Day	SFMW882 07
Hazell Dean	Whatever I Do (Wherever I Go)	SFMW915 03

Artist	Title	Code
Hazell Dean	Who's Leaving Who	SFMW885 09
Heart	Barracuda	SFMW899 03
Heart	These Dreams	SFMW924 13
Heather Small	Proud	SFMW865 07
Heaven 17	Come Live With Me	SFMW844 02
Helen Reddy	Angie Baby	SFMW801 14
Herman's Hermits	Can't You Hear My Heartbeat	SFMW877 11
Hi Gloss	You'll Never Know	SFMW832 13
High Numbers	Zoot Suit	SFMW897 10
High School Musical	We're All In This Together	SFMW926 15
High School Musical	What I've Been Looking For	SFMW928 15
High School Musical 2	Everyday	SFMW929 14
Hoku	Perfect Day	SFMW875 03
Hollies	Carrie Ann	SFMW895 12
Hooters	Satellite	SFMW879 07
Hootie And The Blowfish	Hold My Hand	SFMW881 05
Hot Chocolate	Emma	SFMW808 15
Hot Chocolate	No Doubt About It	SFMW825 07
House Martins	Happy Hour	SFMW830 05
House Of Pain	Jump Around	SFMW850 02
Howard Jones	Like To Get To Know You Well	SFMW832 05
Howard Jones	Little Bit Of Snow	SFMW826 01

Artist	Song	Code
Howard Jones	New Song	SFMW830 11
Howard Jones	Things Can Only Get Better	SFMW908 02
Howard Keel	Bless Your Beautiful Hide	SFMW905 11
Howard Keel	Higher Than A Hawk (Deeper Than A W	SFMW908 14
Hue And Cry	Labour Of Love	SFMW835 15
Huey Lewis	Lonely Teardrops	SFMW866 04
Huey Lewis And The News	Hip To Be Square	SFMW805 14
Huey Lewis And The News	If This Is It	SFMW814 06
Human League	Sound Of The Crowd	SFMW869 07
Ian Dury And The Blockheads	Sex And Drugs And Rock And Roll	SFMW808 06
Ian Dury And The Blockheads	Sweet Gene Vincent	SFMW926 12
Ian Dury And The Blockheads	What A Waste	SFMW857 15
Ian Hunter	Once Bitten Twice Shy	SFMW926 09
Ian Van Dahl	I Can't Let You Go	SFMW848 13
Imagination	Flashback	SFMW844 05
Imelda May	Mayhem	SFMW930 08
Incubus	Drive	SFMW854 09
Indeep	Last Night A Dj Saved My Life	SFMW838 11
Infernal	Self Control	SFMW900 14
Inspiral Carpets	I Want You	SFMW877 05
Inxs	Listen Like Thieves	SFMW869 08

Artist	Title	Code
Inxs	Never Tear Us Apart	SFMW860 03
Inxs	Original Sin	SFMW867 14
Iron Maiden	2 Minutes To Midnight	SFMW889 02
Iron Maiden	Can I Play With Madness	SFMW881 01
Iron Maiden	Evil That Men Do	SFMW888 01
Iron Maiden	Iron Fist	SFMW892 04
Iron Maiden	Number Of The Beast	SFMW880 01
Isaac Hayes	Theme From Shaft	SFMW872 02
Isley Brothers	Shout	SFMW827 02
Isley Brothers	This Old Heart Of Mine	SFMW801 03
It Bites	Calling All The Heroes	SFMW842 01
Italian Job	Self Preservation Society	SFMW882 04
Jace Everett	I Wanna Do Bad Things With You	SFMW931 01
Jack Johnson	Good People	SFMW875 01
Jack Johnson	Upside Down	SFMW877 04
Jack Jones	Impossible Dream	SFMW836 13
Jack Jones	Love Boat	SFMW894 10
Jack Jones	Wives And Lovers	SFMW819 04
Jackie Deshannon	What The World Needs Now Is Love	SFMW819 03
Jackie Lee	White Horses	SFMW881 08
Jackie Trent	Make It Easy On Yourself	SFMW819 05
Jackson 5	I'll Be There	SFMW917 09

Artist	Title	Code
Jacksons	Blame It On The Boogie	SFMW878 09
Jacksons	Can You Feel It	SFMW830 02
Jam	Billy Hunt	SFMW909 02
Jam	In The City	SFMW906 04
Jam	Mr Clean	SFMW908 06
Jam	To Be Someone	SFMW898 06
James	Born Of Frustration	SFMW900 02
James	Fred Astaire	SFMW858 09
James	Runaground	SFMW881 06
James	Say Something	SFMW877 07
James	Sound	SFMW887 07
James Blunt	No Bravery	SFMW906 08
James Brown	Get Up Offa That Thing	SFMW896 04
James Brown	I Got You (Ifeel Good)	SFMW824 07
James Brown	It's A Man's Man's World	SFMW807 08
James Brown	Papa's Got A Brand New Bag	SFMW931 08
James Brown	Sex Machine	SFMW805 11
Jamie Cullum	Frontin	SFMW852 08
Jamiroquai	Cosmic Girl	SFMW846 05
Jane Childs	I Don't Wanna Fall In Love	SFMW843 03
Jane Wiedlin	Rush Hour	SFMW888 06

Artist	Title	Code	Track
Jane's Addiction	Been Caught Stealing	SFMW875	10
Jane's Addiction	Superhero	SFMW908	05
Janet Jackson	Black Cat	SFMW833	03
Janet Jackson And Luther Vand	Best Things In Life Are Free	SFMW812	08
Japan	I Second That Emotion	SFMW831	07
Japan	Quiet Life	SFMW832	08
Japan	Visions Of China	SFMW927	07
Jason Donovan	Too Many Broken Hearts	SFMW930	10
Jeff Buckley	Grace	SFMW859	06
Jeff Buckley	Last Goodbye	SFMW866	02
Jeff Healey	Confidence Man	SFMW828	02
Jennifer Ellison	Baby I Don't Care	SFMW840	01
Jennifer Rush	Power Of Love	SFMW862	05
Jerry Reed	Eastbound And Down	SFMW929	11
Jesse Maccartney	Beautiful Soul	SFMW874	07
Jessica Simpson And Ashlee Si	Little Drummer Boy	SFMW858	08
Jet	Are You Gonna Be My Girl	SFMW850	14
Jet	Get Me Outta Here	SFMW860	04
Jet	Put Your Money Where Your Mouth Is	SFMW885	06
Jimi Hendrix Experience	Foxy Lady	SFMW872	03
Jimi Jameson	I'm Always Here (Baywatch Theme)	SFMW920	09

Artist	Title	Code	Track
Jimmy Buffett	Margaritaville	SFMW918	10
Jimmy Cliff	Wonderful World Beautiful People	SFMW857	12
Jimmy Durante	Make Someone Happy	SFMW911	07
Jimmy Eat World	Middle	SFMW928	09
Jimmy James And The Vagabonds	Now Is The Time	SFMW813	02
Jimmy Nail	Ain't No Doubt	SFMW807	05
Jimmy Nail	Big River	SFMW816	12
Jimmy Nail Tim Healy And Kevi	Blaydon Races	SFMW921	05
Jimmy Ruffin	I'll Say Forever My Love	SFMW818	14
Jimmy Ruffin	What Becomes Of The Broken Hearted	SFMW916	06
Jimmy Somerville	Never Can Say Goodbye	SFMW821	11
Jo Dee Messina	Bye Bye	SFMW917	08
Jo Dee Messina	My Give A Damn's Busted	SFMW891	12
Jo Jo Gunne	Run Run Run	SFMW910	01
Joan Armatrading	Drop The Pilot	SFMW868	03
Joan Armatrading	Love And Affection	SFMW903	11
Joe Dolan	Make Me An Island	SFMW858	07
Joe Esposito	You're The Best	SFMW923	02
Joe Jackson	Is She Really Going Out With Him	SFMW821	12
Joe South	Games People Play	SFMW821	13
Joe Walsh	Life Of Illusion	SFMW905	03

Artist	Song	Code
John Cafferty	Hearts On Fire	SFMW877 03
John Cougar Mellencamp	Jack And Diane	SFMW862 01
John Denver	Leaving On A Jet Plane	SFMW924 04
John Denver	Rocky Mountain High	SFMW887 14
John Denver	Some Days Are Diamonds	SFMW867 05
John Denver	Take Me Home Country Roads	SFMW802 10
John Holt	Help Me Make It Through The Night	SFMW866 05
John Holt	I'll Take A Melody	SFMW848 05
John Holt	Mr Bojangles	SFMW845 04
John Legend	Ordinary People	SFMW869 01
John Lennon	Ballad Of John And Yoko	SFMW813 13
John Lennon	Beautiful Boy (Darling Boy)	SFMW824 11
John Michael Montgomery	I Swear	SFMW813 10
Johnny Cash	25 Minutes To Go	SFMW846 15
Johnny Cash	Big River	SFMW848 06
Johnny Cash	Boy Named Sue	SFMW874 02
Johnny Cash	Cocaine Blues	SFMW923 14
Johnny Cash	Folsom Prison Blues	SFMW879 14
Johnny Cash	Hurt	SFMW891 15
Johnny Cash	I Walk The Line	SFMW889 15
Johnny Cash	One Piece At A Time	SFMW820 12

Artist	Title	Code
Johnny Cash	Ring Of Fire	SFMW815 06
Johnny Cash	San Quentin	SFMW847 06
Johnny Cash	Word Called Love	SFMW835 03
Johnny Hates Jazz	Shattered Dreams	SFMW866 11
Johnny Hates Jazz	Turn Back The Clock	SFMW814 05
Johnny Mathis	Begin The Beguine	SFMW823 04
Jonathan King	Una Paloma Blanca	SFMW872 11
Joni Mitchell	Big Yellow Taxi	SFMW890 09
Joni Mitchell	Both Sides Now (2000 Version)	SFMW892 12
Joni Mitchell	California	SFMW829 04
Josh Dubovie	That Sounds Good To Me	SFMW927 12
Josh Groban	February Song	SFMW901 13
Josh Turner	All Over Me	SFMW930 14
Joshua Radin	I'd Rather Be With You	SFMW925 10
Journey	Don't Stop Believin'	SFMW917 13
Joy Division	Love Will Tear Us Apart	SFMW825 06
Joy Division	Transmission	SFMW913 10
Joyce Sims	All And All	SFMW832 01
Joyce Sims	Come Into My Life	SFMW832 04
Judas Priest	Breaking The Law	SFMW892 01
Judas Priest	Living After Midnight	SFMW893 15

Artist	Title	Code	Track
Julee Cruise	Falling	SFMW911	12
Juliana Hatfield	My Sister	SFMW915	11
Julie Andrews	Lonely Goatherd	SFMW908	08
Julie Andrews	My Favourite Things	SFMW907	16
Julio Iglesias And Willie Nel	To All The Girls I've Loved Before	SFMW819	08
Jurassic 5	Concrete Schoolyard	SFMW883	07
K C And The Sunshine Band	Please Don't Go	SFMW832	07
K C And The Sunshine Band	Shake Shake Shake Shake	SFMW827	05
K7	Come Baby Come	SFMW854	02
Kaiser Chiefs	Everyday I Love You Less And Less	SFMW865	12
Kansas	Carry On Wayward Son	SFMW875	06
Karyn White	Superwoman	SFMW884	13
Kasabian	Cut Off	SFMW861	01
Kate Bush	Army Dreamers	SFMW898	02
Kate Bush	Babooshka	SFMW835	14
Kate Bush	Cloudbusting	SFMW879	04
Kate Bush	Hounds Of Love	SFMW868	10
Kate Bush	Love And Anger	SFMW913	04
Kate Bush	Man With The Child In His Eyes	SFMW895	15
Kate Bush	Running Up That Hill	SFMW837	08
Kate Bush	Sensual World	SFMW896	11

Artist	Title	Code
Kate Bush	This Woman's Work	SFMW899 12
Kate Bush	Wow	SFMW900 05
Kate Hudson ('nine' Soundtrac	Cinema Italiano	SFMW921 10
Kathy Young And The Innocents	Thousand Stars	SFMW876 10
Katie Melua	Closest Thing To Crazy	SFMW850 01
Katie Melua	Flood	SFMW927 06
Katie Melua	My Aphrodisiac Is You	SFMW859 04
Keane	Better Than This	SFMW910 03
Keane	Somewhere Only We Know	SFMW850 15
Kelly Clarkson	Miss Independent	SFMW849 09
Kelly Marie	Feels Like I'm In Love	SFMW802 14
Ken Dodd	Happiness	SFMW821 14
Kenny Loggins	Danger Zone	SFMW859 09
Kid Creole And The Coconuts	Annie I'm Not Your Daddy	SFMW870 14
Kid Rock-feat -sheryl Crow	Picture	SFMW930 05
Kids From Fame	Hi Fidelity	SFMW841 04
Kids From Fame	Starmaker	SFMW842 02
Kiki Dee	Star	SFMW828 11
Killers	All These Things That I've Done	SFMW862 08
Killers	Mr Brightside	SFMW863 01
Kim Wilde	Chequered Love	SFMW896 08

Artist	Title	Code	#
Kim Wilde	Four Letter Word	SFMW869	10
Kim Wilde	You Came	SFMW866	15
Kings Of Leon	Molly's Chambers	SFMW868	13
Kingsmen	Louie Louie	SFMW895	05
Kirsty Maccoll	England 2 Columbia 0	SFMW878	07
Kirsty Mccall	In These Shoes	SFMW870	13
Kiss	God Gave Rock And Roll To You	SFMW816	01
Kiss	I Love It Loud	SFMW879	06
Kiss	Lick It Up	SFMW881	03
Kiss	Strutter	SFMW927	13
Kooks	Naive	SFMW876	03
Korgis	Everybody's Got To Learn Sometime	SFMW871	15
Kraftwerk	Model	SFMW840	12
Kris Kristofferson	Me And Bobby Mcgee	SFMW851	04
Kristian Leontinou	Shining	SFMW856	01
Kristian Leontiou	Story Of My Life	SFMW853	13
Kristin Chenoweth-and-idina M	What Is This Feeling?	SFMW932	15
Kt Tunstall	Black Horse And The Cherry Tree	SFMW863	12
Kt Tunstall	Suddenly I See	SFMW870	02
Kylie Minogue And Jason Donov	Especially For You	SFMW804	05
Kym Sims	Too Blind To See It	SFMW837	06

Artist	Song	Code
Kyu Sakamoto	Sukiyaki	SFMW824 06
La Roux	Quicksand	SFMW915 04
Labi Siffre	Something Inside So Strong	SFMW817 01
Lady Antebellum	Hello World	SFMW932 14
Lady Gaga	Speechless	SFMW925 14
Landscape	Einstein A Go Go	SFMW845 06
Larry Graham	Sooner Or Later	SFMW899 10
Lasgo	Something	SFMW839 06
Lauren Hill	Oh Happy Days	SFMW843 09
Lauren Hill	That Thing You Do	SFMW847 03
Lazlo Bane	Superman	SFMW910 05
Leann Rimes	Blue	SFMW821 15
Led Zeppelin	Mist Mountain Hop	SFMW839 09
Led Zeppelin	Whole Lotta Love	SFMW804 10
Leftfield And Lydon	Open Up	SFMW880 05
Lemonheads	Into Your Arms	SFMW915 10
Lemonheads	Mrs Robinson	SFMW869 06
Lena Zavarone	Ma He's Making Eyes At Me	SFMW843 06
Lenny Kravitz	Always On The Run	SFMW872 06
Lenny Kravitz	Heaven Help	SFMW825 14
Leo Sayer	Thunder In My Heart	SFMW874 04

Artist	Title	Code
Leona Lewis	Footprints In The Sand	SFMW912 12
Leona Lewis	Stop Crying Your Heart Out	SFMW920 03
Les Miserables	Do You Hear The People Sing?	SFMW901 09
Level 42	Almost There	SFMW909 13
Level 42	Hot Water	SFMW921 15
Level 42	Living It Up	SFMW865 04
Levellers	Just The One	SFMW881 10
Libertines	Don't Look Back Into The Sun	SFMW856 08
Lifehouse	Hanging By A Moment	SFMW862 11
Lil Kim	Whoa	SFMW905 10
Limahl	Never Ending Story	SFMW811 15
Linda Ronstadt	When Will I Be Loved	SFMW925 13
Lindisfarne	Run For Home	SFMW832 09
Lindsey Buckingham	Trouble	SFMW867 03
Linkin Park	Faint	SFMW853 10
Linkin Park	Numb	SFMW863 10
Linkin Park	Waiting For The End	SFMW930 02
Lion King	Hakuna Matata	SFMW871 07
Lionel Richie	Angel	SFMW843 15
Lionel Richie	Ballerina Girl	SFMW836 07
Lionel Richie	Dancing On The Ceiling	SFMW852 14
Lionel Richie	Do It To Me	SFMW818 09

Artist	Title	Code
Lionel Richie	Running With The Night	SFMW869 11
Lionel Richie	You Are	SFMW836 08
Lionel Ritchie	Destiny	SFMW866 08
Liquid Gold	Dance Yourself Dizzy	SFMW832 10
Lisa Loeb And Nine Stories	Stay	SFMW839 08
Lisa Stansfield	In All The Right Places	SFMW848 08
Lisa Stansfield	Real Thing	SFMW802 08
Little Richard	Girl Can't Help It	SFMW931 06
Liverpool Express	Every Man Must Have A Dream	SFMW884 03
Living Color	Love Rears It's Ugly Head	SFMW825 13
Living In A Box	Living In A Box	SFMW891 03
Lloyd Cole And The Commotions	Lost Weekend	SFMW837 02
Lobo	I'd Love You To Want Me	SFMW807 11
London Boys	London Nights	SFMW812 02
Lonestar	Amazed	SFMW802 01
Long Pigs	On And On	SFMW908 07
Lonnie Donegan	Jack O' Diamonds	SFMW887 09
Lonnie Donegan	Rock Island Line	SFMW843 10
Look	I Am The Beat	SFMW878 02
Lost Prophets	Last Train Home	SFMW870 11
Lou Reed	Satellite Of Love	SFMW858 14

Artist	Title	Code
Louis Armstrong	We Have All The Time In The World	SFMW867 01
Loverboy	Heaven In Your Eyes	SFMW912 06
Loverboy	Notorious	SFMW906 03
Lulu	To Sir With Love	SFMW886 11
Luniz	I Got 5 On It	SFMW863 13
Lupe Fiasco	Kick Push	SFMW879 08
Luther Vandross	Dance With My Father	SFMW855 04
Luther Vandross	I Really Didn't Mean It	SFMW833 06
Lynyrd Skynyrd	Free Bird	SFMW928 02
Lynyrd Skynyrd	Sweet Home Alabama	SFMW850 06
Lyte Funky Ones	Summer Girls	SFMW875 15
M	Pop Muzik	SFMW828 10
Mac And Katie Kissoon	Sugar Candy Kisses	SFMW883 03
Madonna	Erotica	SFMW824 01
Madonna	Express Yourself	SFMW875 05
Madonna	Express Yourself	SFMW885 15
Madonna	Hanky Panky	SFMW892 15
Madonna	Live To Tell	SFMW824 02
Madonna	Open Your Heart	SFMW893 10
Madonna	Santa Baby	SFMW918 16
Madonna	Vogue	SFMW845 07

Artist	Title	Code
Madonna	Who's That Girl	SFMW807 02
Maisonettes	Heartache Avenue	SFMW874 11
Mama's And Papa's	Creeque Alley	SFMW818 03
Mama's And Papa's	Dream A Little Dream Of Me	SFMW818 05
Mama's And Papa's	Monday Monday	SFMW818 13
Man 2 Man Meets Man Parish	Male Stripper	SFMW891 08
Manic Street Preachers	Motorcycle Emptiness	SFMW843 08
Mansun	Wide Open Space	SFMW873 05
Marc Almond	Days Of Pearly Spencer	SFMW868 15
Mari Wilson	Just What I Always Wanted	SFMW899 14
Maria Lawson	Sleepwalking	SFMW881 12
Mariah Carey	All In Your Mind	SFMW831 01
Mariah Carey	Dreamlover	SFMW872 07
Mariah Carey	Someday	SFMW829 09
Mariah Carey	You Need Me	SFMW829 15
Marillion	Incommunicado	SFMW897 15
Marillion	Lavender	SFMW898 01
Marillion	Sugar Mice	SFMW904 14
Marillion	Warm Wet Circles	SFMW903 08
Marilyn Manson	Beautiful People	SFMW883 04
Marilyn Monroe	Diamonds Are A Girl's Best Friend	SFMW902 06

Artist	Title	Code
Marilyn Monroe	I'm Through With Love	SFMW904 11
Marilyn Monroe	My Heart Belongs To Daddy	SFMW909 11
Marina And The Diamonds	Hollywood	SFMW922 05
Marina And The Diamonds	I Am Not A Robot	SFMW927 10
Mario Lanza	Drink Drink Drink	SFMW902 05
Mario Winans	Never Really Was	SFMW856 15
Maroon 5	Harder To Breathe	SFMW855 05
Marshall Hain	Dancing In The City	SFMW872 04
Martha-and-the Muffins	Echo Beach	SFMW928 05
Martika	Toy Soldier	SFMW846 08
Marty Robbins	Devil Woman	SFMW835 05
Marvelettes	Beechwood 45789	SFMW894 12
Marvelettes	Playboy	SFMW899 05
Marvelettes	When You're Young And In Love	SFMW898 05
Marvin Gaye	Got To Give It Up	SFMW881 13
Mary J Blige	Family Affair	SFMW824 09
Mary J Blige	Going Down	SFMW858 10
Mary J Blige And U2	One	SFMW876 07
Mary Johnson	I'll Pick A Rose For My Rose	SFMW817 13
Massive Attack	Karmacoma	SFMW892 07
Massive Attack	Protection	SFMW893 12

Artist	Title	Code
Massive Attack	Teardrop	SFMW891 10
Massive Attack	Unfinshed Sympathy	SFMW874 14
Matt Bianco	Get Out Of Your Lazy Bed	SFMW831 06
Matt Monro	From Russia With Love	SFMW885 13
Matt Monro	We're Gonna Change The World	SFMW880 10
Matt Willis	Don't Let It Go To Waste	SFMW884 09
Mavericks	All You Do Is Bring Me Down	SFMW848 09
Max Bygraves	Gilly Gill Ossenfeffer	SFMW846 04
Maxine Nightingale	Right Back Where We Started From	SFMW830 15
Mc Hammer	U Can't Touch This	SFMW831 14
Meat Loaf	Blind As A Bat	SFMW884 10
Meat Loaf	Heaven Can Wait	SFMW876 15
Meat Loaf	Life Is A Lemon And I Want My Mone	SFMW882 09
Meat Loaf	Modern Girl	SFMW904 02
Meat Loaf	Read 'em And Weep	SFMW811 08
Mel And Kim	Showing Out	SFMW910 13
Mel C	Yeh Yeh Yeh	SFMW844 13
Mel Torme	Comin' Home Baby	SFMW929 09
Melanie	Ruby Tuesday	SFMW802 11
Melba Moore	This Is It	SFMW822 08
Menswear	Daydreamer	SFMW894 04

Artist	Song	Code
Mental As Anything	Live It Up	SFMW860 12
Merle Haggard	Branded Man	SFMW914 01
Metallica	Enter Sandman	SFMW852 11
Metallica	Wherever I May Roam	SFMW927 01
Mgmt	Electric Feel	SFMW905 13
Miami Sound Machine	Doctor Beat	SFMW834 03
Michael Ball	One Step Out Of Time	SFMW826 14
Michael Ball	With One Look	SFMW842 08
Michael Bolton	Sould Provider	SFMW826 15
Michael Buble	Everything	SFMW899 04
Michael Buble	Heartache Tonight	SFMW923 13
Michael Jackson	Beat It	SFMW861 04
Michael Jackson	Ben	SFMW907 14
Michael Jackson	Billie Jean	SFMW849 02
Michael Jackson	Dirty Diana	SFMW888 02
Michael Jackson	Don't Stop Till You Get Enough	SFMW845 13
Michael Jackson	Farewell My Summer Love	SFMW914 11
Michael Jackson	Liberian Girl	SFMW914 16
Michael Jackson	Man In The Mirror	SFMW838 13
Michael Jackson	One Day In Your Life	SFMW824 10
Michael Jackson	Pyt (Pretty Young Thing)	SFMW920 14
Michael Jackson	She's Out Of My Life	SFMW840 06

Artist	Title	Code
Michael Jackson	She's Out Of My Life	SFMW841 16
Michael Jackson	Stranger In Moscow	SFMW922 11
Michael Jackson	They Don't Really Care About Us	SFMW803 10
Michael Jackson	Thriller	SFMW840 05
Michael Jackson	Way You Make Me Feel	SFMW889 07
Michael Nesmith	Rio	SFMW876 11
Michael Sembello	Maniac	SFMW807 06
Michelle Branch-and-sheryl Cr	Love Me Like That	SFMW931 07
Michelle Pfieffer	Cool Rider (Grease 2)	SFMW920 15
Mick Jagger And Joss Stone	Lonely This Christmas	SFMW857 04
Midge Ure	If I Was	SFMW812 06
Mike And The Mechanics	Over My Shoulder	SFMW802 06
Mike Flowers Pops	Wonderwall	SFMW883 14
Mike Oldfield	Moonlight Shadow	SFMW809 05
Mike Oldfield	Shadow On The Wall	SFMW914 07
Milli Vanilli	Girl You Know It's True	SFMW814 03
Millie	My Boy Lollipop	SFMW814 02
Miranda Lambert	More Like Her	SFMW922 13
Miss Li	Bourgeois Shangri La	SFMW918 03
Mixtures	Pushbike Song	SFMW903 04
Mobiles	Drowning In Berlin	SFMW831 04

Artist	Title	Code	Track
Mock Turtles	Can U Dig It	SFMW879	02
Modern Talking	You're My Heart You're My Soul	SFMW922	07
Monkees	Hey Hey We're The Monkees	SFMW826	09
Montell Jordan	This Is How We Do It	SFMW843	13
Morcheeba	Trigger Hippie	SFMW915	05
Morecambe And Wise	Bring Me Sunshine	SFMW842	11
Morris Albert	Feelings	SFMW901	10
Morrissey	Everyday Is Like Sunday	SFMW870	08
Morrissey	Irish Blood English Heart	SFMW852	05
Morrissey	Let Me Kiss You	SFMW857	09
Morrissey	Suedehead	SFMW856	10
Motels	Total Control	SFMW824	15
Mother Love Bone	Stardog Champion	SFMW908	04
Motorhead	Jailbait	SFMW869	14
Mr Big	Romeo	SFMW867	02
Mr Mister	Kyrie	SFMW833	08
Mud	Cat Crept In	SFMW822	01
Mud	Secrets That You Keep	SFMW822	02
Mumford-and-sons	Winter Winds	SFMW929	04
Mundy	Galway Girl	SFMW915	14
Muse	Neutron Star Collision (Love Is For	SFMW927	02

Artist	Title	Code
Muse	Plug In Baby	SFMW860 01
Muse	Resistance	SFMW931 14
Muse	Sing For Absolution	SFMW853 01
Muse	Time Is Running Out	SFMW856 04
Musical Youth	Pass The Dutchie	SFMW842 15
My Chemical Romance	I'm Not Okay	SFMW867 06
N E R D	Everyone Nose (All The Girls Standi	SFMW906 06
N Trance	Staying Alive	SFMW851 14
Nancy Sinatra	You Only Live Twice	SFMW878 11
Nancy Sinatra And Lee Hazelwo	Jackson	SFMW929 10
Nat King Cole	When I Fall In Love	SFMW887 13
Natalie Cole	Miss You Like Crazy	SFMW808 13
Natasha Bedingfield	I Wanna Have Your Babies	SFMW891 09
Natasha Bedingfield	Say It Again	SFMW898 13
Nazareth	Bad Bad Boy	SFMW874 05
Nazareth	Broken Down Angel	SFMW879 10
Nazareth	Love Hurts	SFMW866 06
N-dubz Feat Mr Hudson	Playing With Fire	SFMW922 06
Ne Yo	Closer	SFMW902 03
Ne Yo	When You're Mad	SFMW906 07
Neil Diamond	Crunchy Granola Suite	SFMW873 14

Artist	Title	Code
Neil Diamond	Hello Again	SFMW835 12
Neil Diamond	Solitary Man	SFMW862 03
Neil Diamond	Summer Love	SFMW904 04
Neil Sedaka	Happy Birthday Sweet Sixteen	SFMW814 14
Neil Sedaka	Laughter In The Rain	SFMW814 13
Neil Sedaka	Miracle Song	SFMW880 14
Nelly	Hot In Here	SFMW848 07
Nelly Furtado	Forca	SFMW856 12
Nelly Furtado	Try	SFMW855 03
Neneh Cherry	Buffalo Stance	SFMW849 12
Neneh Cherry	Manchild	SFMW881 09
New Edition	Candy Girl	SFMW842 03
New Edition	Mr Telephone Man	SFMW900 10
New Order	Blue Monday	SFMW868 06
New Order	Krafty	SFMW864 07
New Order	Regret	SFMW889 08
New Order	True Faith	SFMW846 03
New Seekers	Look What They've Done To My Song	SFMW827 01
Nick Cave And Kylie Minogue	Where The Wild Roses Grow	SFMW862 13
Nick Straker Band	Walk In The Park	SFMW891 04
Nickelback	Rockstar	SFMW895 13

Artist	Song	Code
Nickelback	Savin' Me	SFMW880 08
Night Ranger	Sister Christian	SFMW873 09
Nik Kershaw	Riddle	SFMW839 15
Nina Simone	Ain't Got No I Got Life	SFMW863 02
Nina Simone	Feeling Good	SFMW900 07
Nina Simone	Just Like A Woman	SFMW931 09
Nina Sky	Move Ya Body	SFMW854 01
Nine Inch Nails	Head Like A Hole	SFMW898 04
Nirvana	Come As You Are	SFMW805 15
Nirvana	Heart Shaped Box	SFMW896 02
Nirvana	Smells Like Teen Spirit	SFMW858 02
Noel Murphy	Murphy And The Bricks	SFMW902 13
Nolans	Attention To Me	SFMW902 09
Nolans	Who Gonna Rock You Now	SFMW898 09
Norah Jones	Come Away With Me	SFMW837 14
Norah Jones	Don't Know Why	SFMW837 15
Oasis	Cigarettes And Alcohol	SFMW869 04
Oasis	Do You Know What I Mean	SFMW875 07
Oasis	Don't Look Back In Anger	SFMW840 13
Oasis	Masterplan	SFMW847 08
Oasis	Slide Away	SFMW802 04
Oasis	Stand By Me	SFMW860 05

Artist	Title	Code
Ocean Color Scene	Riverboat Song	SFMW834 12
Odyssey	Going Back To My Roots	SFMW911 04
Offspring	Original Prankster	SFMW807 14
O'jays	Brandy	SFMW917 05
Oleta Adams	Get Here	SFMW850 08
Olivia Newton John	Little More Love	SFMW879 15
Omar	There's Nothing Like This	SFMW856 09
Omd	Forever Live And Die	SFMW914 04
Omd	Locomotion	SFMW873 08
Omd	Tesla Girls	SFMW870 15
Opus	Life Is Life	SFMW838 15
Osmonds	I Can't Stop	SFMW907 08
Outkast	Hey Ya	SFMW849 01
Ozzy Osbourne	Dreamer	SFMW844 04
P M Dawn	Set Adrift On Memory Bliss	SFMW859 15
Paloma Faith	New York	SFMW918 07
Panic At The Disco	I Write Sins Not Tragedies	SFMW886 09
Paolo Nutini	Candy	SFMW917 03
Paolo Nutini	Last Request	SFMW878 06
Paolo Nutini	Ten Out Of Ten	SFMW927 11
Pasadenas	I'm Doing Fine Now	SFMW806 15

Artist	Title	Code
Pasadenas	Tribute (Right On)	SFMW908 10
Pat Benatar	All Fired Up	SFMW888 12
Pat Benatar	Hit Me With Your Best Shot	SFMW899 02
Pat Benatar	Love Is A Battlefield	SFMW875 04
Pat Boone	Speedy Gonzales	SFMW815 05
Patrick Mcknee And Honour Bla	Kinky Boots	SFMW848 14
Patrick Swayze	She's Like The Wind	SFMW804 13
Patsy Cline	Back In Baby's Arms	SFMW868 12
Patsy Cline	I Fall To Pieces	SFMW812 10
Patsy Cline	She's Got You	SFMW815 04
Patsy Cline	Sweet Dreams	SFMW860 15
Patti Austin And James Ingram	Baby Come To Me	SFMW846 11
Patty Smyth	Because The Night	SFMW875 13
Paul And Paula	Hey Paula	SFMW805 02
Paul Evans	Hello This Is Joannie	SFMW913 03
Paul Les And Mary Ford	Vaya Con Dios	SFMW895 14
Paul Mccartney	Frog Chorus	SFMW826 06
Paul Mccartney	Helen Wheels	SFMW906 15
Paul Mccartney	Hi Hi Hi	SFMW900 01
Paul Mccartney	No More Lonely Nights	SFMW816 11
Paul Mccartney	Once Upon A Long Ago	SFMW870 01
Paul Mccartney	Pipes Of Peace	SFMW838 14

Artist	Song	Code	#
Paul Mccartney	Silly Love Songs	SFMW813	12
Paul Mccartney	Tug Of War	SFMW896	06
Paul Mccartney	Wonderful Christmastime	SFMW930	17
Paul Mccartney And M Jackson	Girl Is Mine	SFMW829	12
Paul Mccartney And Stevie Won	Ebony And Ivory	SFMW916	14
Paul Simon	You Can Call Me Al	SFMW853	04
Paul Weller	Thinking Of You	SFMW858	06
Paul Weller	You Do Something To Me	SFMW809	08
Paul Young	Come Back And Stay	SFMW834	02
Paula Cole	I Don't Want To Wait	SFMW839	07
Pearl Jam	Alive	SFMW886	10
Pearl Jam	Daughter	SFMW859	12
Pearl Jam	Even Flow	SFMW901	01
Pearl Jam	Fixer	SFMW917	12
Pearl Jam	Jeremy	SFMW854	14
Pearl Jam	Just Breathe	SFMW922	02
Peggy Lee	Fever	SFMW841	01
Pendulum	Propane Nightmares	SFMW901	02
Pendulum	Watercolour	SFMW925	01
Pet Shop Boys	Did You See Me Coming?	SFMW919	04
Pet Shop Boys	Go West	SFMW811	04

Artist	Song	Code	Track
Pet Shop Boys	It's A Sin	SFMW807	01
Pet Shop Boys And Dusty Sprin	What Have I Done To Deserve This	SFMW836	15
Peter Cetera	Glory Of Love	SFMW806	09
Peter Cetera	Hard To Say I'm Sorry	SFMW808	14
Peter Gabriel	Games Without Frontiers	SFMW865	02
Peter Gabriel	Red Rain	SFMW915	01
Peter Gabriel	Solsbury Hill	SFMW909	06
Peter Gabriel	Steam	SFMW931	03
Peter Gabriel And Kate Bush	Don't Give Up	SFMW847	14
Peter Murphy	Cuts You Up	SFMW913	01
Peter Paul And Mary	Puff The Magic Dragon	SFMW840	08
Peter Skellern	You're A Lady	SFMW903	09
Peter Wylie	Sinful	SFMW871	13
Petula Clark	I Couldn't Live Without Your Love	SFMW836	14
Phantom Of The Opera	All I Ask Of You	SFMW806	08
Phantom Planet	California	SFMW858	05
Phil Collins	Don't Lose My Number	SFMW846	07
Phil Collins	Groovy Kind Of Love	SFMW888	14
Phil Collins	One More Night	SFMW827	09
Phil Collins	Sussudio	SFMW870	04
Phil Collins	Two Hearts	SFMW809	11
Phil Collins And Phil Bailey	Easy Lover	SFMW828	04

Artist	Title	Code
Pikketywitch	That Same Old Feeling	SFMW822 06
Pink	18 Wheeler	SFMW886 01
Pink	Glitter In The Air	SFMW924 05
Pink	I Don't Believe You	SFMW919 10
Pink	There You Go	SFMW882 16
Pink	You Make Me Sick	SFMW885 14
Pink Floyd	Another Brick In The Wall	SFMW848 10
Pink Floyd	Arnold Layne	SFMW897 09
Pink Floyd	Bike	SFMW920 10
Pink Floyd	Breathe	SFMW842 04
Pink Floyd	Great Gig In The Sky	SFMW912 15
Pink Floyd	Have A Cigar	SFMW911 01
Pink Floyd	Mother	SFMW841 12
Pink Floyd	See Emily Play	SFMW918 08
Pink Floyd	Us And Them	SFMW910 12
Pink Floyd	Wish You Were Here	SFMW866 07
Pinkee	Danger Games	SFMW870 07
Piranhas	Where Is My Mind	SFMW857 05
Pirates Of Penzance	Major-general's Song	SFMW899 06
Pixie Lott	Broken Arrow	SFMW929 07
Pixie Lott	Turn It Up	SFMW928 06

Artist	Title	Code
Pixies	Monkey Gone To Heaven	SFMW843 07
Pj And Duncan	Let's Get Ready To Rhumble	SFMW831 09
Placebo	Bitter End	SFMW841 08
Placebo	Nancy Boy	SFMW885 04
Platters	Great Pretender	SFMW924 12
Platters	Only You	SFMW923 12
Player	Baby Come Back	SFMW914 12
Pogues	Dirty Old Town	SFMW867 09
Poison	Every Rose Has It's Thorn	SFMW808 12
Police	Every Little Thing She Does Is Magi	SFMW812 05
Pop Will Eat Itself	Can U Dig It	SFMW863 06
Porno For Pyros	Pets	SFMW902 04
Power Station	Some Like It Hot	SFMW916 15
Prefab Sprout	King Of Rock And Roll	SFMW825 12
Prefab Sprout	When Love Breaks Down	SFMW909 05
Presidents Of The Usa	Lump	SFMW894 07
Presidents Of The Usa	Video Killed The Radio Star	SFMW913 11
Pretenders	Don't Get Me Wrong	SFMW806 12
Pretenders	Hymn To Her	SFMW865 10
Pretenders	Stand By You	SFMW843 11
Pretenders	Talk Of The Town	SFMW914 13
Pretty Reckless	Light Me Up	SFMW929 13

Artist	Title	Code	Track
Pretty Reckless	Make Me Wanna Die	SFMW928	13
Primal Scream	Movin' On Up	SFMW915	06
Primal Scream	Rocks	SFMW854	04
Primitives	Crash	SFMW864	10
Prince	Little Red Corvette	SFMW846	09
Prince	Money Don't Matter 2 Night	SFMW860	09
Prince	Raspberry Beret	SFMW907	11
Proclaimers	I'm On My Way	SFMW824	14
Proclaimers	Sunshine On Leith	SFMW837	01
Psychedelic Furs	Pretty In Pink	SFMW847	11
Python Lee Jackson	In A Broken Dream	SFMW872	09
Q Lazarus	Goodbye Horses	SFMW917	06
Quarterflash	Harden My Heart	SFMW902	10
Queen	Days Of Our Lives	SFMW835	16
Queen	Fat Bottomed Girls	SFMW907	15
Queen	Innuendo	SFMW807	04
Queen	Love Of My Life	SFMW921	09
Queen	One Vision	SFMW852	06
Queen	Princes Of The Universe	SFMW896	01
Queen	Seven Seas Of Rhye	SFMW811	07
Queen	Sheer Heart Attack	SFMW899	09

Artist	Title	Code
Queen	Spread Your Wings	SFMW891 01
Queen	Thank God It's Christmas	SFMW858 01
Queens Of The Stone Age	No One Knows	SFMW866 14
R Dean Taylor	There's A Ghost In My House	SFMW878 12
R Kelly	I Believe I Can Fly	SFMW861 03
Rachel Stevens	Some Girls	SFMW857 07
Radiohead	Paranoid Android	SFMW809 09
Radiohead	There There	SFMW838 07
Rainbow	All Night Long	SFMW905 01
Rainbow	I Surrender	SFMW916 02
Ramones	I Wanna Be Satisfied	SFMW926 04
Ramones	I Wanted Everything	SFMW910 02
Ramones	Rock 'n' Roll High School	SFMW864 13
Randy Crawford	Last Night At Danceland	SFMW918 09
Randy Crawford	Rainy Night In Georgia	SFMW899 08
Rasmus	In The Shadows	SFMW851 01
Ray Charles	I've Got A Woman	SFMW932 11
Razerlight	Golden Touch	SFMW874 03
Razorlight	Vice	SFMW862 10
Rebel Mc	Street Tuff	SFMW861 14
Red Box	For America	SFMW885 08
Red Box	Lean On Me	SFMW883 02

Artist	Title	Code
Red Hot Chili Peppers	Blood Sugar Sex Magik	SFMW882 11
Red Hot Chili Peppers	Scar Tissue	SFMW848 01
Red Hot Chili Peppers	Suck My Kiss	SFMW883 10
Rem	Stand	SFMW906 05
Reo Speedwagon	Can't Fight This Feeling	SFMW849 05
Reparata And The Delrons	Captain Of Your Ship	SFMW890 11
Reynolds Girls	I'd Rather Jack	SFMW891 05
Rhian Benson	Say How I Feel	SFMW857 11
Richard Marx	Angelia	SFMW829 01
Richard Marx	Love Unemotional	SFMW830 09
Richard Marx	Now And Forever	SFMW829 08
Rick Derringer	I Am A Real American	SFMW917 14
Rick James	Superfreak	SFMW880 12
Rick Springfield	Human Touch	SFMW900 03
Rick Springfield	Jessie's Girl	SFMW873 10
Ricky Martin	Saint Tropez	SFMW815 10
Rihanna	Pon De Replay	SFMW886 07
Ringo Starr	It Don't Come Easy	SFMW818 07
Ringo Starr	Photograph	SFMW816 15
Roachford	Family Man	SFMW912 05
Roachford	Way I Feel	SFMW833 14

Artist	Title	Code
Robbie Robertson	Somewhere Down The Crazy River	SFMW888 15
Robbie Williams	Hot Fudge	SFMW863 04
Robbie Williams	Man For All Seasons	SFMW841 02
Robbie Williams	She's Madonna	SFMW886 12
Robert Palmer	Bad Case Of Loving You	SFMW840 09
Robert Palmer	Every Kind Of People	SFMW845 03
Robert Plant	29 Palms	SFMW913 02
Robert Plant And Alison Kraus	Let Your Loss Be Your Lesson	SFMW911 09
Robert Plant And Alison Kraus	Please Read The Letter	SFMW912 09
Robert Tepper	No Easy Way Out	SFMW883 12
Robin Beck	First Time	SFMW851 06
Robyn	Dancing On My Own	SFMW926 06
Rod Stewart	Sailing	SFMW862 14
Rod Stewart	Some Guys Have All The Luck	SFMW852 04
Rod Stewart	You Wear It Well	SFMW861 07
Rodriguez	Sugarman	SFMW855 10
Roger Daltrey	Giving It All Away	SFMW873 13
Roger Whitaker	Don't Believe In Is Anymore	SFMW813 01
Rogue Traders	Voodoo Child	SFMW878 08
Rogue Traders	Watching You	SFMW881 07
Rolf Harris	Court Of King Caractacus	SFMW844 03
Rolf Harris	Stairway To Heaven	SFMW853 09

Artist	Title	Code
Rolf Harris	Two Little Boys	SFMW851 13
Rolling Stones	Brown Sugar	SFMW820 05
Rolling Stones	I Can't Get No Satisfaction	SFMW856 06
Rolling Stones	It's All Over Now	SFMW813 14
Rolling Stones	Jumpin' Jack Flash	SFMW870 12
Rolling Stones	Last Time	SFMW802 09
Rolling Stones	Sympathy For The Devil	SFMW858 13
Romantics	What I Like About You	SFMW872 01
Ron Moody (Oliver! Soundtrack)	Reviewing The Situation	SFMW916 11
Ronan Keating And Brian Kenne	Now That I Know What I Want	SFMW872 08
Ronnie Lane	How Come	SFMW928 10
Rooster	Come Get Some	SFMW856 05
Rose Royce	Car Wash	SFMW807 13
Roxette	Dressed For Success	SFMW804 09
Roxette	Joyride	SFMW808 11
Roxette	Look	SFMW811 03
Roxy Music	Avalon	SFMW832 02
Roxy Music	Dance Away	SFMW907 13
Roxy Music	Love Is The Drug	SFMW853 03
Roxy Music	More Than This	SFMW809 04
Roxy Music	Over You	SFMW832 06

Artist	Title	Code
Roy Orbison	California Blue	SFMW854 12
Roy Orbison	Communication Breakdown	SFMW803 12
Roy Orbison	Leah	SFMW873 11
Roy Orbison	Love So Beautiful	SFMW837 04
Roy Orbison	Penny Arcade	SFMW867 15
Roy Orbison	She's A Mystery To Me	SFMW883 08
Roy Orbison	You Got It	SFMW882 14
Ruby And The Romantics	Our Day Will Come	SFMW827 12
Rufus Wainwright	Hallelujah	SFMW845 02
Rupert Holmes	Escape (The Pina Colada Song)	SFMW837 03
Rush	Closer To The Heart	SFMW905 15
Rush	Spirit Of Radio	SFMW921 01
Rush	Turn The Page	SFMW902 01
Russell Watson	Where My Heart Will Take Me	SFMW842 13
Rutles	Cheese And Onions	SFMW912 08
Rutles	Knicker Elastic King	SFMW911 13
Rutles	Questionnaire	SFMW910 04
Ryan Paris	Dolce Vita	SFMW902 07
S Club 7	Stand By You	SFMW815 15
S O S Band	Finest	SFMW842 06
S O S Band	Just Be Good To Me	SFMW839 03
S W F	Flowers	SFMW802 03

Artist	Title	Code
Sad Cafe	Every Day Hurts	SFMW875 14
Sade	By Your Side	SFMW877 14
Sade	Sweetest Taboo	SFMW816 14
Sade	Your Love Is King	SFMW823 15
Sailor	Girls Girls Girls	SFMW863 09
Salt 'n' Pepa	Push It	SFMW888 13
Sam Brown	Stop	SFMW811 02
Sam Cooke	Twistin The Night Away	SFMW855 14
Sam The Man And The Pharaohs	Wooly Bully	SFMW816 08
Sandra	I'll Never Be Maria Magdalena	SFMW922 04
Santana And The Product	Maria Maria	SFMW805 10
Santogold	Les Artistes	SFMW901 12
Sarah Maclachlan	Angel	SFMW895 09
Sarah Mclachlan	Drifting	SFMW914 15
Sarah Mclachlan	Full Of Grace	SFMW844 07
Sarah Mclachlan	I Love You	SFMW897 05
Sarah Michelle Gellar	Going Through The Motions	SFMW887 01
Saturdays	Ego	SFMW920 12
Savage Garden	Affirmation	SFMW804 02
Saxon	Wheels Of Steel	SFMW842 05
Sciissor Sisters	Comfortably Numb	SFMW872 13

Artist	Title	Code
Scissor Sisters	Laura	SFMW855 01
Scissor Sisters	Take Your Mama	SFMW852 02
Scott Walker	Joanna	SFMW817 15
Screaming Trees	Nearly Lost You	SFMW913 13
Scritti Politti	Absolute	SFMW910 06
Scritti Politti	Wood Beez	SFMW915 02
Scritti Politti	Word Girl	SFMW887 10
Seahorses	Love Is The Law	SFMW887 12
Sean Kingston	Beautiful Girls	SFMW892 10
Secret Affair	Time For Action	SFMW878 05
Seekers	Georgy Girl	SFMW894 05
Seekers	When Will The Good Apples Fall	SFMW910 07
Seether And Amy Lee	Broken	SFMW858 04
Selecter	On My Radio	SFMW882 05
Serge Gainsbourg And Jane Bir	Je T'aime (Moi Non Plus)	SFMW900 06
Shakespear's Sister	Stay	SFMW845 05
Shakespear's Sister	You're History	SFMW907 05
Shakin' Stevens	Green Door	SFMW834 06
Shakin' Stevens	Oh Julie	SFMW840 15
Shakin' Stevens	This Ole House	SFMW833 15
Sham 69	Angels With Dirty Faces	SFMW893 06
Sham 69	Borstal Breakout	SFMW889 04

Artist	Title	Code
Sham 69	Hersham Boys	SFMW890 05
Sham 69	If The Kids Are United	SFMW892 02
Shamen	Boss Drum	SFMW885 03
Shamen	Eberneezer Goode	SFMW831 08
Shamen	L S I	SFMW883 06
Shangri Las	Remember (Walking In Thesand)	SFMW869 12
Shania Twain	Any Man Of Mine	SFMW906 09
Shania Twain	Honey I'm Home	SFMW815 02
Shania Twain	No One Needs To Know	SFMW836 10
Shania Twain	Thank You Baby	SFMW849 15
Shania Twain	What Made You Say That	SFMW836 09
Sharleen Spiteri	All The Times I Cried	SFMW906 12
Shed Seven	Chasing Rainbows	SFMW869 09
Shed Seven	She Left Me On A Friday	SFMW834 13
Shelby Lynn	Tell Me I'm Crazy	SFMW871 14
Sheryl Crow	First Cut Is The Deepest	SFMW852 01
Sheryl Crow	If It Makes You Happy	SFMW812 09
Sheryl Crow	Run Baby Run	SFMW809 15
Shinedown	If You Only Knew	SFMW922 01
Shirley Bassey	Kiss Me Honey Honey Kiss Me	SFMW835 13
Shirley Bassey	Moonraker	SFMW884 15

Artist	Title	Code
Shirley Bassey	Thank You For The Years	SFMW900 08
Shirley Bassey	This Is My Life	SFMW919 14
Shirley Bassey And The Propel	History Repeating	SFMW869 15
Shirley Jones	Till There Was You (From The Music	SFMW913 07
Shirley Temple	Animal Crackers In My Soup	SFMW904 10
Shirley Temple	On The Good Ship Lollipop	SFMW903 12
Simon And Garfunkel	Bridge Over Troubled Water	SFMW864 01
Simple Minds	Love Song	SFMW916 01
Simple Minds	Waterfront	SFMW829 13
Simply Red	Fairground	SFMW802 05
Simply Red	For Your Babies	SFMW806 10
Simply Red	Money's Too Tight	SFMW806 11
Simply Red	So Beautiful	SFMW871 10
Simpsons	Do The Bart Man	SFMW831 03
Sinitta	Toy Boy	SFMW905 06
Siobhan Donaghy	Overrated	SFMW840 03
Siouxsie And The Banshees	Dear Prudence	SFMW839 01
Siouxsie And The Banshees	Peek a-boo	SFMW888 11
Sir Mix A Lot	Baby Got Back	SFMW897 07
Sisters Of Mercy	Lucrecia My Reflection	SFMW891 07
Sisters Of Mercy	This Corrosion	SFMW889 01
Skunk Anansie	Brazen	SFMW905 02

Artist	Title	Code
Skunk Anansie	Weak	SFMW865 05
Slade	Cum On Feel The Noize	SFMW889 13
Slade	Get Down Get With It	SFMW913 09
Slade	Take Me Back 'ome	SFMW813 09
Sleeper	Inbetweener	SFMW894 06
Small Faces	All Or Nothing	SFMW818 10
Smash Mouth	Walking On The Sun	SFMW841 15
Smashing Pumpkins	Today	SFMW917 07
Smiths	Heaven Knows I'm Miserable Now	SFMW853 07
Smiths	There Is A Light That Never Goes Ou	SFMW839 12
Smokie And Suzie Quatro	Stumblin' In	SFMW808 03
Snap	Power	SFMW861 05
Sneaker Pimps	6 Underground	SFMW882 08
Snow Patrol	Run	SFMW850 03
Snow Patrol	You Could Be Happy	SFMW912 10
Soft Cell	Say Hello Wave Goodbye	SFMW825 09
Soggy Bottom Boys	I Am A Man Of Constant Sorrow	SFMW908 15
Soho	Hippy Chick	SFMW877 06
Solomon Burke	Cry To Me	SFMW864 11
Sophie B Hawkins	Damn I Wish I Was Your Lover	SFMW833 05
Soundgarden	Black Hole Sun	SFMW874 09

Artist	Title	Code
Soundgarden	Rusty Cage	SFMW903 01
Soundgarden	Spoonman	SFMW884 08
Soundgarden	Superunknown	SFMW890 01
Source Feat Candi Staton	You Got The Love	SFMW874 01
Space	Female Of The Species	SFMW856 14
Space	Me And You Versus The World	SFMW894 02
Space	Neighbourhood	SFMW892 11
Spacehog	In The Meantime	SFMW912 14
Spagna	Call Me	SFMW890 10
Spandau Ballet	Only When You Leave	SFMW814 08
Spandau Ballet	Through The Barricades	SFMW807 07
Sparks	Beat The Clock	SFMW818 11
Specials	Ghost Town	SFMW806 14
Spice Girls	Who Do You Think You Are	SFMW867 13
Spitting Image	Chicken Song	SFMW835 04
St Etienne	He's On The Phone	SFMW884 11
Stacey Orrico	More To Life	SFMW847 05
Staind	Epiphany	SFMW841 10
Staind	It's Been A While	SFMW845 08
Stakka Bo	Here We Go	SFMW879 05
Stan Ridgway	Camouflage	SFMW870 09
Standard	My Grandfather's Clock	SFMW820 11

Artist	Title	Code	Track
Standard	When You Wish Upon A Star	SFMW803	06
Stanley Holloway	Any Old Iron	SFMW909	08
Starland Vocal Band	Afternoon Delight	SFMW903	15
Starsailor	Fever	SFMW841	06
Starsailor	Four To The Floor	SFMW854	06
Starship	We Built This City	SFMW855	08
Status Quo	Ice In The Sun	SFMW803	08
Status Quo	Paper Plane	SFMW912	13
Status Quo	Wild Side Of Life	SFMW801	08
Steely Dan	Haitian Divorce	SFMW859	03
Steely Dan	Reelin' In The Years	SFMW932	08
Stephen Tintin Duffy	Kiss Me	SFMW884	06
Stereophonics	Everyday I Think Of Money	SFMW826	05
Stereophonics	Madame Helga	SFMW838	10
Steve Harley	Here Comes The Sun	SFMW834	07
Steve Winwood	Valerie	SFMW861	13
Stevie Nicks	Rooms On Fire	SFMW897	12
Stevie Nicks	Talk To Me	SFMW836	04
Stevie Wonder	Don't You Worry About A Thing	SFMW830	03
Stevie Wonder	Lately	SFMW826	11
Stevie Wonder	Ribbon In The Sky	SFMW916	12

Artist	Title	Code
Stevie Wonder	Signed Sealed Delivered I'm Yours	SFMW915 13
Sting	Feilds Of Gold	SFMW806 02
Sting	It's Probaly Me	SFMW839 13
Sting And Mary J Blige	Whenever I Say Your Name	SFMW848 02
Stone Sour	Inhale	SFMW843 05
Stone Temple Pilots	Plush	SFMW890 02
Stone Temple Pilots	Vasoline	SFMW884 07
Stranglers	Nice And Sleazy	SFMW880 02
Stranglers	No More Heroes	SFMW886 04
Stranglers	Skin Deep	SFMW883 01
Stranglers	Strange Little Girl	SFMW879 09
Strawberry Switchblade	Since Yeasterday	SFMW909 12
Streets	Don't Mug Yourself	SFMW860 08
Strokes	Juicebox	SFMW873 02
Strokes	Last Night	SFMW835 09
Style Council	Long Hot Summer	SFMW832 14
Style Council	Only To Be With You	SFMW861 10
Style Council	You're The Best Thing	SFMW832 12
Su Pollard	Starting Together	SFMW907 07
Suede	Animal Nitrate	SFMW895 06
Suede	Beautiful Ones	SFMW848 15
Suede	Trash	SFMW932 04

Artist	Title	Code
Sugar	If I Can't Change Your Mind	SFMW912 02
Sugar Minnott	We've Got A Good Thing Going	SFMW850 09
Sugarhill Gang	Rappers Delight	SFMW873 01
Sugarland	All I Want To Do	SFMW930 13
Sugarland	Baby Girl	SFMW892 09
Sugarland	Stuck Like Glue	SFMW928 11
Sundays	Cry	SFMW909 10
Sundays	Here's Where The Story Ends	SFMW905 08
Sundays	Summertime	SFMW903 14
Sundays	Wild Horses	SFMW889 09
Sunscreem	Love You More	SFMW903 02
Supertramp	Bloody Well Right	SFMW884 05
Supertramp	Breakfast In America	SFMW876 04
Supertramp	Give A Little Bit	SFMW875 11
Supertramp	Logical Song	SFMW873 04
Supremes	Stoned Love	SFMW812 14
Supremes	You Keep Me Hangin' On	SFMW895 11
Survivor	Burning Heart	SFMW904 01
Susan Boyle	Don't Dream It's Over	SFMW932 05
Susan Boyle	End Of The World	SFMW922 10
Susan Boyle	I Dreamed A Dream	SFMW917 11

Artist	Title	Code
Susan Boyle	Perfect Day	SFMW931 10
Susan Boyle	Proud	SFMW921 02
Susanna	In The Heat Of The Night	SFMW925 07
Sutherland Bros	Lying In The Arms Of Mary	SFMW805 06
Suzanne Vega	Luka	SFMW811 12
Suzanne Vega	Marlene On The Wall	SFMW916 10
Suzanne Vega	Tom's Diner	SFMW895 02
Suzi Quatro	If You Can't Give Me Love	SFMW822 03
System Of A Down	Toxicity	SFMW930 04
T Rex	Children Of The Revolution	SFMW005 13
T Rex	Metal Guru	SFMW813 06
T Rex	Telegram Sam	SFMW811 10
Take That	Million Love Songs	SFMW815 07
Take That	S O S	SFMW932 13
Take That And Lulu	Relight My Fire	SFMW816 09
Taken By Trees	Sweet Child O' Mine	SFMW919 12
Talk Talk	It's My Life	SFMW904 03
Talk Talk	Life's What You Make It	SFMW859 11
Talk Talk	Talk Talk	SFMW843 12
Talking Heads	And She Was	SFMW884 04
Talking Heads	Once In A Lifetime	SFMW866 03
Tams	Hey Girl Don't Bother Me	SFMW813 07

Artist	Title	Code	Track
Tanita Tikaram	Good Tradition	SFMW862	04
Taylor Swift	Back To December	SFMW932	16
Taylor Swift	Jump Then Fall	SFMW919	06
Taylor Swift	Speak Now	SFMW930	15
Tears For Fears	Head Over Heels	SFMW850	11
Tears For Fears	Mad World	SFMW831	11
Tears For Fears	Sowing The Seeds Of Love	SFMW811	05
Technotronic	Pump Up The Jam	SFMW805	01
Teddy Bears	To Know Him Is To Love Him	SFMW827	13
Temple Of The Dog	Hunger Strike	SFMW913	12
Temptations	Get Ready	SFMW916	07
Temptations	Treat Her Like A Lady	SFMW923	08
Temptations	You're My Everything	SFMW924	08
Tenacious D	Tribute	SFMW849	10
Tenacious D	Wonderboy	SFMW843	14
Terence Trent D'arby	Sign Your Name	SFMW852	09
Terence Trent D'arby	Wishing Well	SFMW807	12
Terence Trent D'arby And Des'	Delicate	SFMW910	11
Terri Walker	Whoopsie Daisy	SFMW863	07
Terry Bush	Maybe Tomorrow	SFMW854	15
Terry Scott	My Brother	SFMW907	09

Artist	Title	Code	#
Terry Wogan	Floral Dance	SFMW895	07
Texas	Can't Resist	SFMW871	12
Texas	Carnival Girl	SFMW848	03
The The	Infected	SFMW880	03
Theme From Mash	Suicide Is Painless	SFMW834	15
Then Jerico	Big Area	SFMW873	12
Therapy	Nowhere	SFMW886	08
Therapy	Screamager	SFMW887	03
They Might Be Giants	Birdhouse In Your Soul	SFMW850	12
Thin Lizzy	Boys Are Back In Town	SFMW804	14
Thin Lizzy	Dancin' In The Moonlight	SFMW887	04
Thin Lizzy	Jailbreak	SFMW863	11
Thin Lizzy	Rocker	SFMW906	01
Thin Lizzy	Rosalie	SFMW896	07
Thin Lizzy	Sarah	SFMW903	03
Thin Lizzy	Waiting For An Alibi	SFMW890	04
Thomas Dolby	She Blinded Me With Science	SFMW878	01
Thompson Twins	Love On Your Side	SFMW830	08
Thompson Twins	We Are Detective	SFMW886	03
Three Degrees	When Will I See You Again	SFMW811	01
Three Degrees	Woman In Love	SFMW913	05
Thrills	Big Sur	SFMW846	13

Artist	Title	Code
Thunder	Better Man	SFMW880 11
Thunder	Dirty Love	SFMW908 01
Thunder	I Love You More Than Rock And Roll	SFMW898 15
Thunder	Love Walked In	SFMW882 06
Thunder	Low Life In High Places	SFMW890 06
Tight Fit	Fantasy Island	SFMW831 05
Tim Mcgraw	Live Like You Were Dying	SFMW853 15
Timbuk 3	Future's So Bright I Gotta Wear Sha	SFMW903 13
Time	Jungle Love	SFMW895 03
Tina Arena	Symphony Of Life	SFMW868 14
Tina Moore	Open Arms	SFMW857 06
Tito And The Tarantulas	After Dark	SFMW917 15
Tobi Legend	Time Will Pass You By	SFMW911 05
Toby Keith	American Soldier	SFMW850 10
Tom Jones	Funny Familiar Forgotten Feeling	SFMW823 03
Tom Jones	You Can Leave Your Hat On	SFMW828 15
Tom Jones And Natalie Imbrugl	Never Tear Us Apart	SFMW830 10
Tom Jones And Robbie Williams	Are You Gonna Go My Way	SFMW829 02
Tom Petty	Free Fallin'	SFMW871 08
Tom Petty	I Won't Back Down	SFMW897 11
Tom Petty And The Heartbreake	American Girl	SFMW923 11

Artist	Title	Code
Tom Petty And The Heartbreake	Don't Come Around Here No More	SFMW886 05
Tom Petty And The Heartbreake	Into The Great Wide Open	SFMW907 02
Tom Petty And The Heartbreake	Learning To Fly	SFMW887 02
Tom Waits	Goin' Out West	SFMW867 10
Tommy Sparks	She's Got Me Dancin'	SFMW920 05
Tommy Steele	Little White Bull	SFMW820 13
Tony Bennett	Fly Me To The Moon (In Other Words)	SFMW925 12
Tony Christie	Avenues And Alleyways	SFMW859 14
Topol	If I Were A Rich Man	SFMW891 13
Toto	Rosanna	SFMW855 12
Toyah	I Want To Be Free	SFMW842 07
T'pau	Valentine	SFMW911 03
Tracie Young	House That Jack Built	SFMW912 07
Tracy Chapman	Fast Car	SFMW847 12
Traditional (Big Band)	Deck The Halls	SFMW918 12
Traditional (Brass Band And C	We Wish You A Merry Christmas	SFMW918 13
Train	Drops Of Jupiter	SFMW847 01
Train	Hey Soul Sister	SFMW927 04
Trammps	Zing Went The Strings Of My Heart	SFMW820 06
Transvision Vamp	Baby I Don't Care	SFMW897 08
Traveling Wilberys	End Of The Line	SFMW851 07
Traveling Wilburys	Heading For The Light	SFMW911 15

Artist	Title	Code
Travelling Wilburys	Handle With Care	SFMW876 14
Travis	Driftwood	SFMW802 02
Travis	Tied To The 90's	SFMW842 12
Tremeloes And Roberta Flack	Me And My Life	SFMW803 07
Trini Lopez	Guantanamera	SFMW901 07
Tubeway Army	Are Friends Electric	SFMW801 05
Tubeway Army	Are Friends Electric	SFMW812 03
Tune Weavers	Happy Happy Birthday Babe	SFMW877 12
Tyketto	Standing Alone	SFMW891 02
U B 40	Don't Break My Heart	SFMW812 12
U B 40	I'll Be Your Baby Tonight	SFMW807 10
U B 40	One In Ten	SFMW812 11
U B 40	Swing Low Sweet Chariot	SFMW847 13
U2	Angel Of Harlem	SFMW813 15
U2	Desire	SFMW876 09
U2	Even Better Than The Real Thing	SFMW850 07
U2	One	SFMW921 08
U2	Until The End Of The World	SFMW864 12
U2	With Or Without You	SFMW837 09
Ultrabeat	Feelin' Fine	SFMW870 10
Ultrabeat	Pretty Green Eyes	SFMW844 14

Artist	Title	Code
Ultravox	All Stood Still	SFMW870 05
Ultravox	Dancing With Tears In My Eyes	SFMW812 13
Ultravox	Hymn	SFMW914 14
Ultravox	Love's Great Adventure	SFMW906 10
Ultravox	Visions In Blue	SFMW913 14
Ultravox	Voice	SFMW862 09
Uriah Heap	Sweet Lorraine	SFMW909 03
Val Doonican	Special Years	SFMW910 09
Van Halen	When It's Love	SFMW888 04
Van Halen	You Really Got Me	SFMW803 13
Van Morrison	Brown Eyed Girl	SFMW838 01
Van Morrison	Moondance	SFMW838 05
Vanessa Williams	Colour Of The Wind	SFMW853 11
Vannessa Paradis	Joe Le Taxi	SFMW825 05
Vaughn Monroe	Ghost Riders In The Sky	SFMW812 04
Velvelettes	He Was Really Saying Somethin'	SFMW918 14
Velvelettes	Needle In A Haystack	SFMW916 09
Velvet Revolver	Fall To Pieces	SFMW866 09
Velvet Underground	I'm Sticking With You	SFMW903 10
Velvet Underground	I'm Waiting For The Man	SFMW854 13
Vera Lynn	We'll Meet Again	SFMW882 18
Verve	Sonnet	SFMW809 10

Artist	Title	Code
Victoria Wood	Ballad Of Barry And Freda	SFMW826 03
View	Superstar Tradesman	SFMW914 02
View	Wasted Little Djs	SFMW908 09
Violent Femmes	Blister In The Sun	SFMW849 14
Visage	Fade To Grey	SFMW832 15
Vv Brown	Shark In The Water	SFMW930 12
Wah	Story Of The Blues	SFMW911 10
Wanda Jackson	Right Or Wrong	SFMW926 05
Wannadies	You And Me Song	SFMW865 09
Warren G And Nate Dogg	Regulate	SFMW868 08
Wayne Newton	Daddy Don't You Walk So Fast	SFMW823 05
Weezer	Buddy Holly	SFMW851 02
Weezer	If You're Wondering If I Want You T	SFMW921 03
Weird Al Yankovic	Ebay	SFMW900 15
Weird Al Yankovic	Men In Brown	SFMW829 06
West Side Story	Maria	SFMW927 15
Westlife	Angels Wings	SFMW815 13
Westlife	Loneliness Knows Me By Name	SFMW815 14
Wet Wet Wet	All I Want	SFMW858 12
Wham	Edge Of Heaven	SFMW921 11
Wham	Everything She Wants	SFMW920 16

Artist	Title	Code
Wham	Freedom	SFMW846 14
Whispers	And The Beat Goes On	SFMW813 04
Whispers	And The Beat Goes On	SFMW831 02
White Plains	Julie Do You Love Me	SFMW813 03
White Stripes	Denial Twist	SFMW932 03
Whitesnake	Ain't No Love In The Heart Of The C	SFMW906 02
Whitesnake	Deeper The Love	SFMW908 03
Whitney Houston	All At Once	SFMW820 08
Whitney Houston	All At Once	SFMW827 03
Whitney Houston	I Believe In You And Me	SFMW813 11
Whitney Houston	Love Will Save The Day	SFMW824 04
Whitney Houston	My Name Is Not Susan	SFMW827 04
Whitney Houston	So Emotional	SFMW880 15
Whitney Houston	Why Does It Hurt So Bad	SFMW824 03
Who	Bell Boy	SFMW921 13
Who	I'm The One	SFMW902 14
Who	My Generation	SFMW855 13
Who	Punk And The Godfather	SFMW922 03
Who	Seeker	SFMW896 03
Wiley	Wot Do You Call It	SFMW851 15
Wilkinsons	26 Cents	SFMW892 14
Wilson Phillips	Hold On	SFMW872 10

Artist	Title	Code
Wings	Band On The Run	SFMW861 06
Wings	Listen To What The Man Said	SFMW823 01
Wolfmother	Back Round	SFMW929 01
Wombats	Let's Dance To Joy Division	SFMW894 14
Wombles	Remember You're A Womble	SFMW830 14
Wonder Stuff	Size Of A Cow	SFMW885 02
Wonderstuff	Welcome To The Cheap Seats	SFMW841 03
X T C	Making Plans For Nigel	SFMW841 07
X T C	Senses Working Overtime	SFMW871 05
X T C	Sgt Rock (Is Going To Help Me)	SFMW907 03
X T C	Towers Of London	SFMW869 05
Yardbirds	For Your Love	SFMW925 04
Yazoo	Nobody's Diary	SFMW826 13
Yello	Race	SFMW888 05
Yes	Lift Me Up	SFMW901 15
Yes	Wonderous Stories	SFMW910 14
Zac Brown Band	Chicken Fried	SFMW928 03
Zac Brown Band	Toes	SFMW919 02
Zero 7	Destiny	SFMW912 04
Zombies	Tell Her No	SFMW845 11
Zutons	Why Don't You Give Me Your Love	SFMW876 01

TozMusic
Karaoke Books

Published by TozMusic

For other karaoke books, please email tozmusic@hotmail.co.uk
we print most karaoke books, all major brands and many more are covered.

We can also print custom made books, if you email us the disc codes

eg. sfmw873

or the disc make and numbers

CPSIA information can be obtained
at www.ICGtesting.com
Printed in the USA
LVOW09s1606071117
555333LV00043B/670/P

9 781544 860510